WILDBOY
TO THE EDGE AND BACK

I was on the brink of being so cold that I wasn't <u>feeling</u> cold anymore.

I realised that I had hypothermia and that I needed to do something, right now.

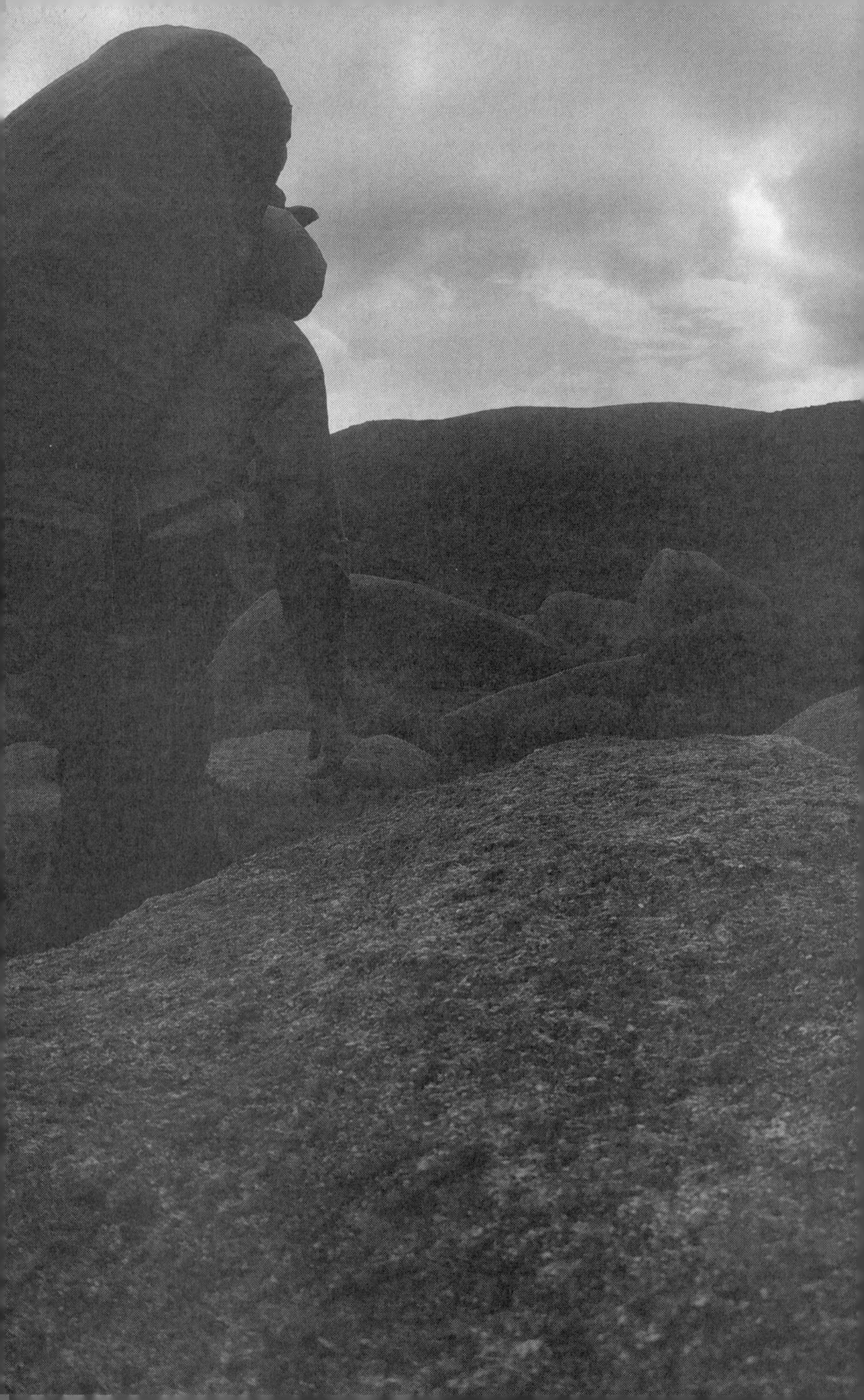

If I didn't, I was going to die.

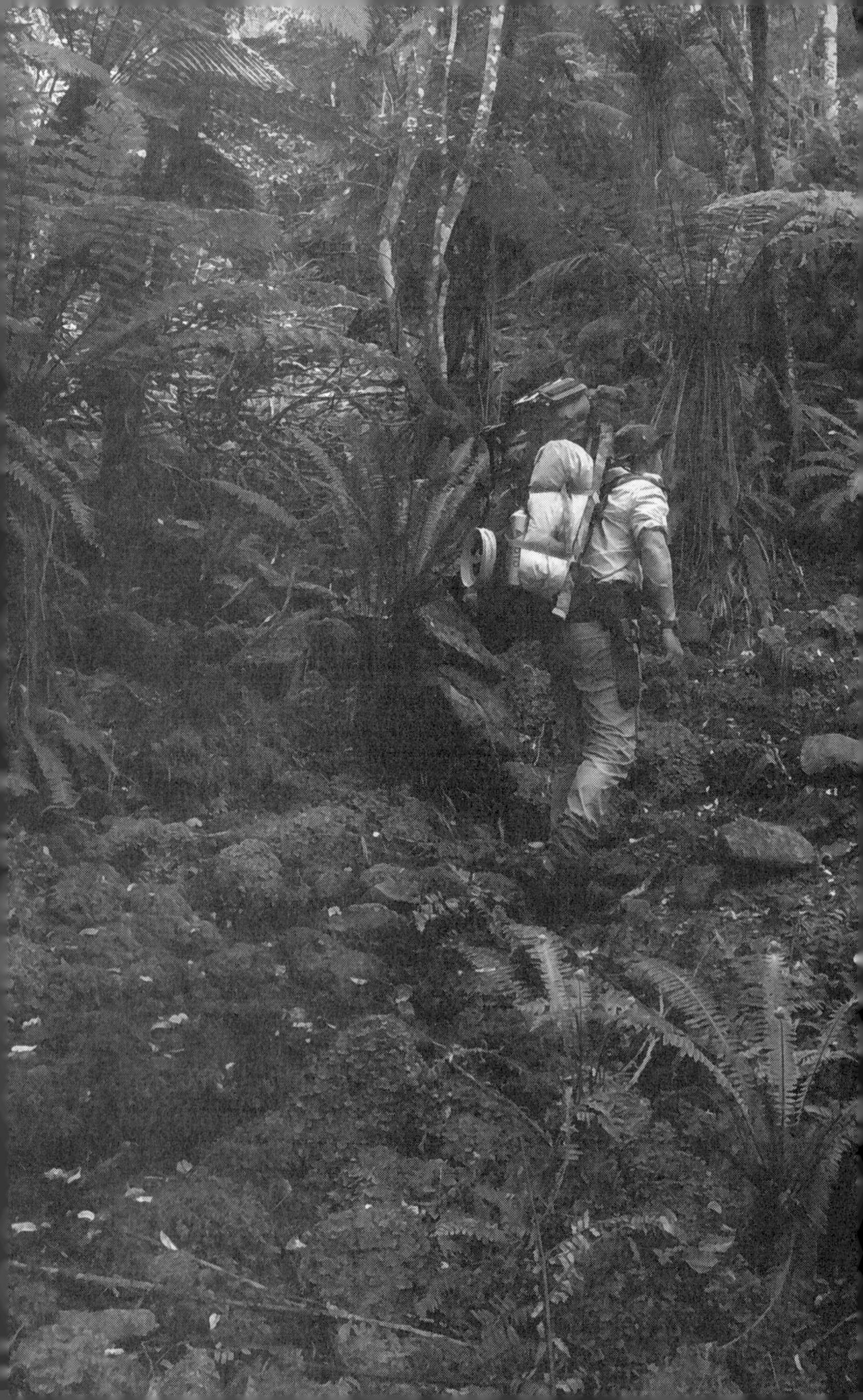

Brando Yelavich
with Nicola McCloy

WILDBOY
TO THE EDGE AND BACK

More adventures through rugged,
remote New Zealand

PENGUIN BOOKS

PENGUIN

UK | USA | Canada | Ireland
Australia | India | New Zealand
South Africa | China

Penguin is an imprint of the Penguin Random House group of companies, whose addresses can be found at global.penguinrandomhouse.com.

Penguin Random House
New Zealand

First published by Penguin Random House New Zealand, 2017

10 9 8 7 6 5 4 3 2 1

Text and photography © Brando Yelavich, 2017

The moral right of Nicola McCloy to be identified as the author has been asserted.

All rights reserved. Without limiting the rights under copyright reserved above, no part of this publication may be reproduced, stored in or introduced into a retrieval system, or transmitted, in any form or by any means (electronic, mechanical, photocopying, recording or otherwise), without the prior written permission of both the copyright owner and the above publisher of this book.

Design and map by Carla Sy
© Penguin Random House New Zealand
Prepress by Image Centre Group
Printed and bound in Australia by Griffin Press, an Accredited ISO AS/NZS 14001 Environmental Management Systems Printer

A catalogue record for this book is available from the National Library of New Zealand.

ISBN 978-0-14-377133-3
eISBN 978-0-14-377134-0

penguin.co.nz

MIX
Paper from responsible sources
FSC® C009448

To everyone living their life to its fullest

Contents

PROLOGUE
16

Chapter One
LIFE AFTER NEW ZEALAND
19

Chapter Two
THE OTHER ISLAND
31

Chapter Three
INTO THE UNKNOWN
49

Chapter Four
DOUBT
91

Chapter Five
STRUGGLE
117

Chapter Six
TURNING POINT
145

Chapter Seven
FACING DEATH
163

Chapter Eight
RELIEF
185

Chapter Nine
COMPANY
207

Chapter Ten
REFLECTION
233

Chapter Eleven
THE FINISH LINE
259

Chapter Twelve
AFTERWARDS
265

Stewart Island

Prologue

Day 17
26.11.16
Tin Range, Stewart Island

As the day wore on, the wind continued to pick up and the rain became more frequent. The higher I climbed, the colder I got. My lack of food meant I became cold quickly — way quicker than normal.

I CARRIED ON UP towards the top of the range. It was pretty flat up there but it was completely exposed. The rain had stopped but the wind was still getting worse.

It was hard to try to stay upright walking through the knee-high scrub. One gust was so strong that it blew me off my feet. To make matters worse, I was up so high that I could see a storm coming. I'd have no real way of sheltering from it. All I could do was keep moving.

Twenty minutes later, I was walking along the ridge. The only positive thing about the wind was that it had dried my clothes. That's when the rain, hail and snow started falling — and it wasn't just falling, it was being forced out of the skies by the gnarly wind. It was coming at me sideways. And I was cold. Really cold.

I had never been in a situation like this before. I was soaked. All my gear was freezing and my hands . . . well, they didn't even work.

At about two o'clock I found a little patch of low bush and sat down next to it. I huddled in a ball. That's when it dawned on me that something was really wrong.

I thought to myself, 'This is kind of weird. Why am I not still walking and keeping warm?' I knew there was something wrong from the fact I was sitting in a bush but I couldn't work out what it was. Then I clicked. It was like 'Woah! I'm really, really cold!' I was so cold that I'd even stopped shivering.

I was on the brink of being so cold that I wasn't *feeling* cold anymore. In a detached way, I realised that I had hypothermia and that I needed to do something, right now. If I didn't, I was going to die.

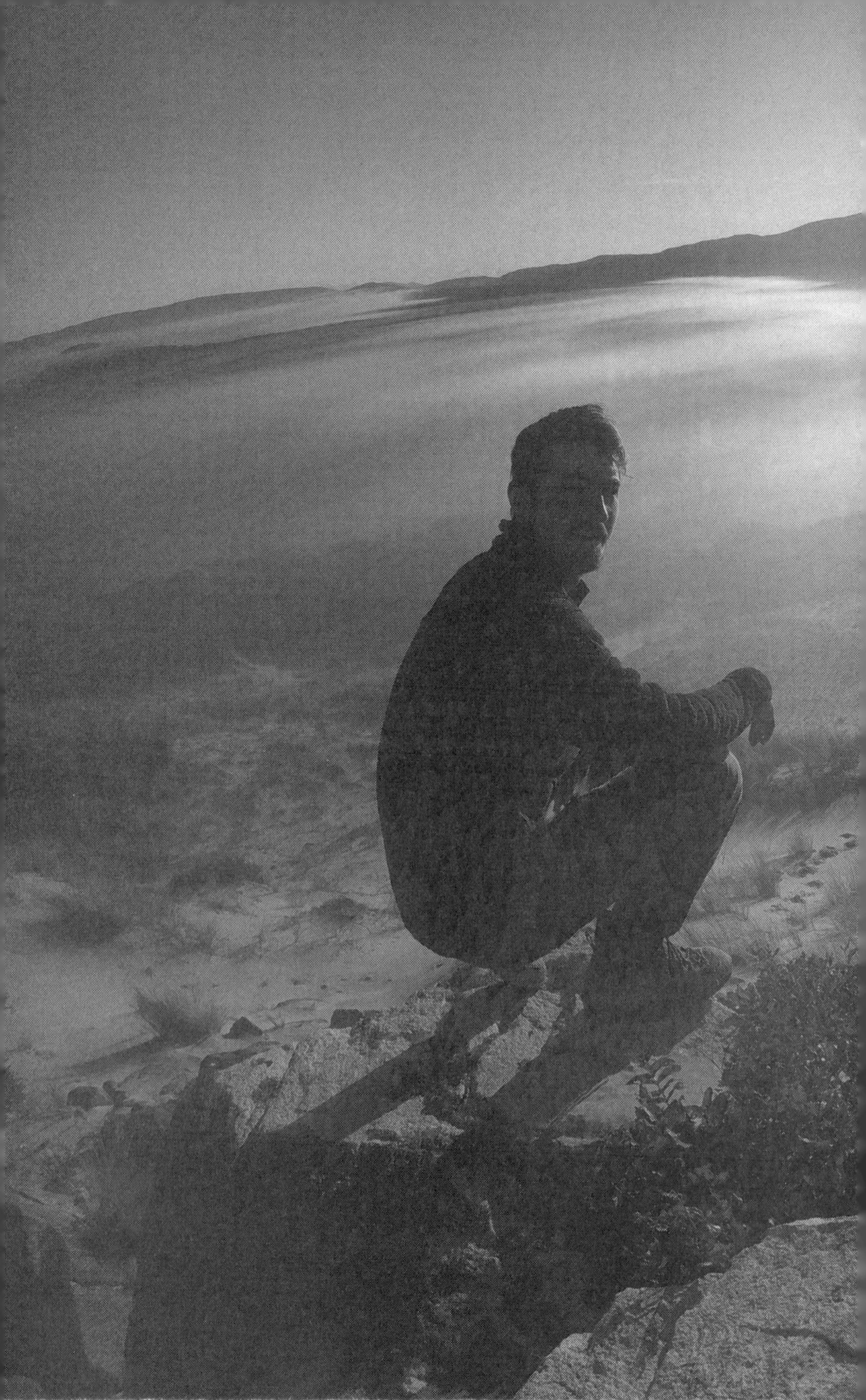

Chapter One
LIFE AFTER NEW ZEALAND

My name is Brando Yelavich, and you may have heard of me. Or maybe not. Sometimes I go by the name of Wildboy. I'm that crazy kid who decided the best way to sort out his life was by walking around New Zealand. Alone. See what I mean by crazy?

I WAS BROUGHT UP on Auckland's North Shore. I really struggled with school, and being diagnosed with ADHD and dyslexia didn't help. Conventional schooling was a huge challenge for me, then my dream of one day joining the army was destroyed due to my learning difficulties. By the time I was in my late teens I was on a roller-coaster ride that was going nowhere good — fast. I felt lost and angry. My relationships with my family, friends and community were at breaking point. I couldn't see any sort of future for myself, so I escaped into drinking and drugs.

It wasn't quite this simple, but basically one day I woke up and decided that I was going to walk around the coast of New Zealand. Having ADHD means that once I set my mind on something, there's no getting away from it. I was completely unprepared for a challenge like this: I had no money, virtually no gear and I figured it would take me about six months. No one believed I could do it — and, to be honest, I'm not sure I really thought I could either. None of that stopped me from setting off from Cape Reinga on 1 February 2013 with a 50-kilogram pack on my back and not much idea about what lay ahead. I was 19 years old and I had nothing better to do than walk — so walk I did.

Over the next 600 days — see, I underestimated the time a little bit — I met the most amazing people, got chased by a few wild dogs, ate a lot of delicious food (and some not-that-delicious food), paddled around the Marlborough Sounds, rafted down rivers, and walked over 8000 kilometres around the coast of this country to land me back where I had started at Cape Reinga on 23 August 2014.

The journey changed me. I overcame near-death situations, incredible loneliness and enormous physical and logistical obstacles. My emotions ran wild, but I had forged a new future for myself. I came back with a completely altered view of the world and my place in it. My relationship with my family had mended and I had met my own Wildgirl, Ngaio, while I was walking around the Coromandel coast. I could finally see a future for myself where before I had none.

HOWEVER, AFTER FINISHING THE round New Zealand trip, it took a lot for me to adjust back to real life. I was so used to just getting up and walking every day that I didn't really know how to do anything else. I went back to Auckland and lived with my family while I tried to work out what I was going to do next.

After a few months of going to the Coromandel to see Ngaio whenever I could, I moved down there to be with her that summer. Things went well for a while. I

The journey changed me. I overcame near-death situations, incredible loneliness and enormous physical and logistical obstacles. My emotions ran wild, but I had forged a new future for myself.

got my truck licence and worked for Ngaio's dad doing deliveries for his plant nursery. I loved it because every day was different — a bit like being out walking.

I got involved in the community. I was part of the local Volunteer Fire Service, I played in a soccer team — I felt like I belonged there.

I had also made really good friends with a guy called Ben. Like me, Ben had a passion for adventure. We got along so well — we were always either on a mission together or planning our next one.

One night, the local fire brigade was having its annual function in Hahei when we got called out to a car accident. It was my first proper emergency.

It was like something out of a movie. One minute everyone was having a great night and we were all happy. Then we got this call-out. We jumped in the truck and headed off down the road.

When we got there, there was a vehicle upside down in the river. I recognised the car right away. Ben had accidentally driven off a bridge. Crew members got into dive gear and jumped into the river, but, tragically, Ben didn't make it. I couldn't believe it. I'd never lost someone close to me and spent the following weeks trying to come to terms with what had happened.

Not long after, things got worse. I was lifting hay bales when I perforated a disc in my back. I was going to have to have surgery to have some of the disc cut off so that it would stop pushing on the nerve and causing me pain. Unfortunately, it was about three months before I got the surgery.

Waiting around, I got really depressed. Ben was gone, and my back injury stopped me from doing things I wanted to do. I was enjoying my job driving trucks — it gave me 'dream time', just like when I was walking — and I was a good worker. But after I hurt my back, I couldn't work very well — physically I could still drive but I was in a lot of pain. I couldn't even sit comfortably in the truck. I couldn't sleep either. I was stuck lying in bed, not able to do anything, and I isolated myself from everyone apart from Ngaio. I was pretty much on my own and it messed my head up real bad.

Eventually, my hospital date came around. Everything went to plan until after the surgery. Unfortunately, when I'm on medication — painkillers like tramadol and things like that — I get really paranoid and start thinking that something bad will happen. Sure enough, I woke up one night in hospital and was convinced that the guy in the bed next to me wanted to kill me.

I snuck out of my bed and crept down the hallway. I was walking down the path outside, trying to escape, when one of the nurses found me and asked what was going on. 'This guy in my room is trying to get me! He's trying to kill me!'

She calmly took me back to the ward, where this other guy was fast asleep, and assured me that they'd protect me. She sat and talked to me for ages until I was calm enough to go to sleep.

Another time when Ngaio came to see me, I was heading towards the window with my laptop tucked under my gown because I was convinced the same guy was trying to steal it. I felt kind of bad because he was such a nice guy. Maybe they should have tied me to the bed!

AFTER THE SURGERY, it was six weeks before I was allowed to start doing anything physical, then I had 10 weeks of physiotherapy and rehabilitation exercises to do — which I probably wasn't as dedicated to as I should have been. It was about six months before I was able to do everything I wanted to again.

This was a real big down patch. I would just watch movies and sit around doing nothing. I struggle to even remember most of it, things were that bad. I kind of disconnected myself from everything. I wouldn't even go outside.

Adjusting to life after the walk around New Zealand would have been hard anyway but those challenges made it so much harder. They were different challenges to what I was used to. Because I had survived the New Zealand walk I knew that I could conquer just about any physical challenge. But these mental challenges, they screwed me up for ages.

During my trip around New Zealand, I had this mindset that every day I had a goal to achieve — and that was to walk. Then suddenly when I didn't have to do anything, I struggled to find meaning in my life. There didn't seem to be any point in even getting out of bed. Ngaio would get home from work and I'd still be lying there — I wouldn't have got up or eaten all day. The first thing I'd say to her is, 'What is there to eat?' I'd be so hungry but I couldn't be bothered actually going and getting food for myself.

It must have been really hard on her. So I think she was a little bit relieved when I told her I was moving to Nelson, as she knew this would give me the best opportunity to be happy.

The whole Nelson thing came about after I started doing a bit of 'coasteering', taking people out on adventures along the coast over summer. I decided I wanted to do something like that career-wise, but I had no idea how to make it happen.

Then I met this awesome guy called Kyle. He's a travel blogger (@barekiwi) who I met through social media. He was coming to the Coromandel, so I offered him a place to stay and for him to come on a coasteering mission with me. He jumped at the chance.

Kyle is a real cool guy. He'd done this two-year certificate in adventure tourism at Nelson Marlborough Institute of Technology (NMIT) in Nelson. He was like, 'You should totally do this course. I know the guy, I'll hook you up.' A couple of weeks later I was gone!

I wanted to do the coasteering thing but I didn't have the knowledge of how to set it up as a business. I could see that this course would give me the skills I needed to build a business out of doing the things I love.

It was great to have a goal to focus on again. I was in Nelson for a reason, doing heaps of cool stuff but ultimately getting the skills I needed to get on with the next stage of my life.

Through the course, I learn the skills I need to be able to work in the outdoors. It's like full-time rock climbing, rafting, kayaking, hiking, you name it. I've

Because I had survived the New Zealand walk I knew that I could conquer just about any physical challenge. But these mental challenges, they screwed me up for ages.

learnt heaps already, met lots of people who like the same things as me, and I've gained lots of new skills. It's quite different getting taught to do things instead of just working out how to do them. It's much easier to master a skill when someone is telling you the right way to do it!

After having spent ages working out how to get around gnarly bits of the coast myself, it took a while for me to learn to do things in a new way. To start with, I got a bit of feedback about being over-confident, but I just put that down to all the experience that I had in the wilderness. I was so used to working alone that I had to learn to be part of a team, which is important because when you're working in the outdoors you'll often be responsible for other people's safety.

I am in my second year now. There are only about 15 days in a classroom this year, but there were more in the first year — it was every Monday. It was a bit weird going back into a classroom situation after the tough time I'd had at school but, fortunately, I found it much easier this time. I think it was because I was learning stuff I really wanted to know about.

When I first went to Nelson, it was really to give me a solid skill set while I worked out what I wanted to do with my life. I figured I could study and learn new skills while I sussed out new adventures, but I got so engaged in the course that didn't really happen. But then I had an idea for another adventure . . .

Being Wildboy

While I was studying at NMIT I was still doing a bit of Wildboy stuff, but I didn't have the chance to go on any more big adventures. I did quite a lot of public speaking for a while, and I still go and talk at schools quite often. I love doing that — it's so cool to see the looks on kids' faces when I tell them my story. I was absolutely stoked that my first book, *Wildboy*, was nominated for the New Zealand Book Awards for Children and Young Adults in 2016 in the readers' choice section. Not bad for someone who struggled with reading and writing!

As well as getting recognised by kids from my school talks, I get recognised from my social media quite a bit. Since my walk around New Zealand, my social media has grown bigger and bigger. I've got my Facebook page — Wildboy Adventures — and my Instagram. They just keep on growing. It's a bit tricky sometimes because I find social media quite challenging. I like that it means people can communicate directly with me — but sometimes it makes it feel a bit hard to be real and I struggle with that. I just have to try to remain true to myself and remember that my public image and who I really am are sometimes two different things.

Chapter Two

THE OTHER ISLAND

In mid-2016, I was sitting on my bed in my room in Nelson, talking to my friend Lucy, telling her about my adventure around the coast of New Zealand. She suddenly said, 'What about Stewart Island?'

OF COURSE, DURING MY round New Zealand journey I'd walked *past* Stewart Island. It's about 30 kilometres south of the South Island, and on a good day, you can see the island from all along the south coast. I remember thinking it was this huge, wild place which would be great to explore, but that I couldn't get to it on that trip. I hadn't thought about it again until Lucy raised it as a possibility.

That got me thinking. I'd already walked around the coast of New Zealand, so maybe I should try to walk around the coast of Stewart Island as well. It would be the wildest place I had ever been. I decided it had to be done!

I had always been drawn to this part of New Zealand. It's the closest you can get to Antarctica without a major boat trip. I knew that if I walked around Stewart Island, at some point I would probably be the southernmost person in New Zealand, and that excited me.

A switch had flicked on in my head that couldn't be switched off. I had my new dream. I had the next adventure. I decided I was going to do it at the end of the year but had no idea how I was going to actually make it happen.

I talked to a few people and, with a lot of help, the plan started to come together. It took about four months to get all my gear together, plot a route and get some sponsors on board. I was so excited. Kathmandu were amazing — they said I could have whatever gear I needed. And then Venture Southland came on board. Their job is to promote tourism in Southland and, as Stewart Island is part of the province, we both thought this would be a great way to get the place some exposure. They put me in touch with Stewart Island Experience and Stewart Island Flights, who also agreed to help me out.

My own planning started with creating a great big map of the island. To make a map big enough for the level of planning I needed to do, I printed out lots of different sections of the topographical map, cut them out and taped them together. My map of the whole island was absolutely huge. I stuck it to the ceiling of my room so every day it was the first and last thing I looked at, when I woke up and before I went to sleep. It was a friendly reminder of my goal, and to keep up the drive to live my dream.

Next, I had to plan my route. I got out my compass, pulled the map off the ceiling and started plotting. My idea was to start in Oban, the only town on the island. I planned to head around the North West Circuit track until I reached the point where it cut inland, which I figured was just under 110 kilometres on foot. From there I was going to be walking into the wild. No tracks, no people, no huts.

I quickly realised the island was way bigger than I originally imagined. It was going to take between 30 and 40 days to travel about 450 kilometres around the whole coast. The thought of carrying 40 days' worth of food was daunting — I had no idea how much it would weigh, but I was sure it would be heavy.

I had an idea, and gave my mates at Absolute Wilderness a call. They agreed to help me out with freeze-dried meals, so I put in a special order for 30 of their 100-gram meals, vacuum-packed as flat as possible so they would fit in my bag and weigh only 3 kilograms. Even with these meals, I'd still have to live off the land quite a bit. On my walk around New Zealand I'd eaten heaps of wild stuff, so I was confident I'd be able to do that here, too, but I decided it would be good to have the pre-prepared meals as a back-up.

Another big part of the planning was making sure I had all the right permissions from the right people. It can sometimes be very scary approaching someone for permission, but 98 per cent of the time — as long as you're doing nothing wrong or destructive — people are more than happy to let you through or onto their land.

The access question was made a bit simpler by the fact that 85 per cent of Stewart Island is a national park, so is run by the Department of Conservation (DOC). I got in touch with them and was told that I'd need a bunch of permits but that I'd be able to sort those out when I got to Oban. I also called the Rakiura Maori Lands Trust, which administers the Maori land on the island, and explained what I was doing. They were happy to help, too.

I had my gear, I had my maps, I had access to the land that I needed to cross. Everything was ready, now I just had to wait . . .

SOMETIMES THIS STAGE CAN be one of the hardest. I needed to focus on finishing my year at NMIT before I could focus on the big adventure that awaited me in the far south of the country. I had three months to get through, but my mind was ready to set off now and get started on this epic adventure.

The closer the departure date got, the more excited I became. I had been into Kathmandu and picked up all my equipment. It was such a cool feeling going into a shop and filling a bag with all the gear I needed, knowing I didn't have to pay for it — kind of like Christmas. I figured that I'd be going away in the middle of summer so I got a lot of summer-weight things: summer-weight sleeping bag, light-weight down jacket and so on. For now, I felt I had everything that I needed.

As well as being excited I was also starting to feel anxious. I knew I was going to be lonely, I knew it was going to be hard. I was worried about being away from my girlfriend for so long, especially because we had spent most of the year apart, with me in Nelson and Ngaio in the Coromandel. I felt bad about then spending a big chunk of my holidays away from her, too.

Apart from being away from Ngaio, this trip would be tough because Stewart Island is so isolated. When I was walking around New Zealand, I was never very far away from people and I knew that I would always be able to restock my supplies every few days. On the island, I would be spending a lot of time by myself. This was going to be one of the most challenging trips of my whole life.

The day before I was due to leave, I was in a bit of a mess. My brain was full of information firing off in every direction, at every moment. I understood what I had to do but everything seemed too much for me. I took a few deep breaths and realised my ADHD brain had got the better of me. I needed to relax, but I couldn't. I was so stressed out about the unknown, and about leaving the civilised world behind. I was worrying about the future and remembering the past. A solo trip taking 30 or 40 days was going to be intense. I had to carry everything I would need with me, to survive any situation I found myself in. On top of that, I needed to carry all the camera gear to capture my adventure, and the technology to charge it.

I was sitting there on the floor of my parents' house in the middle of a big pile of gear having a total meltdown. I had all the gear I needed — I had it sprawled out all over the floor in front of me. Packing is my least favourite thing to do, but this was even worse than usual — I had no motivation to pack the gear into my bag. Inside my head was this dark fear that I would never return to the real world if I went on this adventure.

But then, I'm not sure I've ever been part of the real world anyway. I came back from walking around New Zealand with a completely changed perspective on life and found I couldn't fit in to what some people call 'normal' society. Would this trip make that worse?

It was such an overwhelming feeling, but I knew I just needed to breathe, and to pack. Breathe and pack. I slowly got my gear together and systematically packed it into my bag. I knew exactly where everything needed to go, and it wasn't long until I had put everything inside my pack and zipped it shut. I went to bed still feeling nervous, knowing that when I woke up in the morning, it was D-day. The trip was all go.

MUM LET ME SLEEP IN — she didn't want to wake me because she knew I had a big day ahead of me. I packed up the last of my gear, hoping that the GoPro I had ordered was going to show up. I had been told it would be delivered in the morning but the couriers couldn't find it.

I waited as long as I could for the courier to arrive, but nothing came. That made me a whole lot more stressed. I rushed to the airport, had a cup of coffee with my mum and said goodbye. Then I was off.

On my flight to Christchurch I ended up sitting in front of a girl who was really angry. I eavesdropped on her conversation. She was on her way to court and must have done something bad because she was talking about what she was going to do when she got out, and I guessed she was meaning jail. She had what I thought were two youth workers with her, who were helping her through the court process. I felt sorry for her that she didn't seem to have much of a support network. I wanted to give her a copy of *Wildboy* and say 'Read this! Go on an adventure!'

Once I got to Christchurch I had a few hours to fill in, so

I went and got a drink of water and posted details about my trip on Instagram (I wouldn't be able to post much for a while, because there's not a lot of cell service on Stewart Island). After waiting for what felt like days, I heard the boarding call for my flight to Invercargill. I was still so nervous. I got picked up on arrival by one of the reps from Venture Southland. She took me to Noel Leeming, where I was able to buy another GoPro, so that I had a spare. I spent a bit of time adding protective lenses to the camera, which would come in handy out in the wild.

She then took me to the Invercargill Top 10 Holiday Park, who put me up for the night in an awesome unit. They also cooked me my last home-cooked meal. It was a delicious roast chicken with potatoes and buttered bread. Eating it, I started to wonder about my choice to carry so little food. Would I have enough? I am a very active person, and because of this I eat a lot of food (plus I love food). During the lead-up to my trip, I had been overeating rather than preparing by cutting back my portions. The thought of the physically demanding days to come, and the fact I'd be living off 100-gram meals, was not too appealing. I realised I should have done things differently.

After that, I went into town with the holiday park owner's daughter, and together we walked along the side of the estuary to see if I could see Stewart Island. But there was too much cloud. It would have been kind of a relief to see it, because it wouldn't be long before I was getting on a little plane and setting off down there.

I felt emotionally confused that night. On one hand,

A switch had flicked on in my head that couldn't be switched off. I had my new dream. I had the next adventure. I was going to be walking into the wild. No tracks, no people, no huts.

I was frothing about the idea of walking around Stewart Island but, on the other, I was terrified. I knew it would be fun but I was setting off into the unknown. I was fit enough because of all the adventure activities I'd been doing and because my lifestyle was very active. I had the mental capacity to do it, because of what I had already achieved. But I felt like I hadn't done enough planning. I'd done all that work on my map, plotting a route, but I didn't feel like I knew enough about the weather or the landscape.

I did my best to silence my doubts. 'That's just how I do things,' I told myself. I had everything I needed to keep myself alive in any situation. Where was the fun in having an adventure where you know where everything is, where you're going to get water, when you're going to have cell service, when you're going to get food? Walking into the unknown is my idea of an adventure. And that was what I was going to do now. I was doing it because I wanted to and because I could, and because I love adventure!

THE NEXT MORNING, I was up at 6.30, all checked in by 7.20 and on the plane at 7.50 — after the obligatory Southland cheese-roll breakfast, of course. It was a bit chilly, with a bit of a breeze, but at least the sun was shining as we left Invercargill.

Once we got airborne, the weather across Foveaux Strait looked a bit grey and cloudy. I hoped that wasn't a sign of things to come.

I was joined by a handful of passengers on the flight

to Stewart Island. It was pretty bumpy up there but thankfully the flight only took 20 minutes.

As I was sitting there with these other people, it felt weird that I had no idea what they were going there to do and they had no idea what I was up to. By the look of it they were mostly tourists going to see Stewart Island. They would probably see the popular sites at Halfmoon Bay and the nature reserve at Ulva Island, then head back to Invercargill. Not me, though — I was going to see a whole lot more. They were all looking at me a bit funny as I had my camera up to the window most of the way.

It's hard to describe how it felt to see the island from the air for the first time. It's like this beautiful green jewel in the middle of the grey ocean. Its beauty was amazing, but seeing just how big the place is made me feel quite nervous. As rain started to splatter on the plane's windows, my doubts rose up again.

At 8.20 a.m. — right on schedule — we touched down on the island. While it was almost summer in the rest of the country, it was still really cold on Stewart Island.

A quick trip in a van and I arrived in Oban. As I got out of the van, I looked up to see the plane I'd just come in on flying back to Invercargill. That's when I realised that I wouldn't be back on the mainland for more than a month. This adventure had just begun.

I spent the night at Bunkers Backpackers, where they checked me into the Hellfire room. That might seem like a weird name, but on Stewart Island, it's not — it's named after Big Hellfire Beach on the western side of the island.

The place was really cool. All the people there were

seasoned travellers who were into having adventures. I met a real mixture of Kiwi travellers and people from overseas.

After dropping off my bags, I headed down to the DOC office to get all my permits sorted out. While I waited to talk to one of the rangers, I checked out a few of the displays. I probably shouldn't have spent so long looking at the one that was all about sharks. I knew there were a lot of great white sharks around the island, but from the display I found out that scientists think they are probably the largest great whites in the world. Excellent!

I also learned that there are six more species of shark in the waters around the island — basking sharks, mako sharks, porbeagle sharks (what even *is* a porbeagle!?), seven-gilled sharks, thresher sharks and blue sharks. I knew that now I'd probably think about them all every time I decided to go for a dive to get paua while I was on the coast.

I had to fill out a whole lot of paperwork in the DOC office before I could walk off into the national park. Because I was filming for commercial purposes, I had to fill out different forms for each location, which was a bit tricky as I wasn't sure where I'd be going.

The DOC staff were super nice to me but getting through all the forms was a bit of a mission. They're not really designed for people who aren't quite sure where they're going, what they'll be doing, how long they'll be doing it for, and what they'll be filming. And they definitely weren't designed for people like me who have dyslexia and find reading quite hard.

I also met a local policeman who said, 'Every time someone comes and tells me they're doing this, I have to come down and talk to them.' Then he told me the story of a German teenager who stole his dad's credit card, flew from Germany to New Zealand and ran off to Stewart Island, with no wilderness experience. He went off for 10 days with two blocks of chocolate and lost his backpack four days in. He showed up at the DOC office so starving that, apparently, he walked past everyone and just started eating the biscuits they had there for morning tea.

Forms filled out and permits approved — except for a possum-hunting permit that I had to go back for — I headed off for a bit of a look around Halfmoon Bay before going back to the backpackers to sort out my stuff for the following day. While I was doing that, I officially named my backpack. I'd been thinking about a name for it for a while and decided that it would be called Stewart Little — even though it wasn't that little (actually it was huge!) given it had all my stuff in it for a long time in the bush.

I met a few locals who were doubtful about what I wanted to do. In the pub, the night before I left, I talked to a guy called Cod-eyes. He showed me a bit of coastline on the map and said, 'I did that. Took me four days.' I thought, 'Four days! It doesn't look that far.'

That evening, as the sun went down, I treated myself to fish and chips down at the beach — my last dinner in civilisation for a while. As I sat looking out on Halfmoon Bay, I had no idea of the challenges that were awaiting me.

Before heading back to my last night in a proper bed, I drew a line in the sand that would serve as my starting point the next day. I'd arrive back at the same point in who-knew-how-many days' time, having walked around the coast of Stewart Island.

Stewart Island — glowing skies

- The Maori name for Stewart Island is Rakiura. It's usually translated to mean 'glowing skies'. Given some of the sunsets I saw on the island, I can see why. Some people reckon it could also be called that because you can see the aurora australis or Southern Lights from the island.
- The island's European name comes from William Stewart, the first officer on the *Pegasus*, a sealing ship that visited from Sydney in 1809.
- The island is about 75 kilometres long and, at its widest point, about 45 kilometres wide.
- It covers an area of 1683 square kilometres. Around 85 per cent of that land area is a national park, which was established in 2002.
- The island has about 400 permanent residents, most of whom live in Oban on Halfmoon Bay and work in fishing, aquaculture and tourism. Oban is the island's only town, and it is named after a town in Scotland.
- The highest point on the island is Mount Anglem, which is 980 metres above sea level.
- The average temperature on the island is 16°C in summer, and 9°C in winter. Not that hot!
- There are only about 28 kilometres of road on the island, but there's more than ten times that number of walking tracks.

Gear list

Here's a list of all the gear I took with me, to last for 30–40 days in the wilderness. My 75-litre pack weighed about 30 kilograms when it was full.

- [ ] 1 x tent
- [ ] 1 x pack liner
- [ ] 30 x 100-gram packets of freeze-dried food
- [ ] 1 x merino shirt
- [ ] 1 x waterproof jacket
- [ ] 2 x pairs merino thermals (top and bottom)
- [ ] 1 x pair of long pants
- [ ] 1 x pair of shorts
- [ ] 2 x pairs of socks
- [ ] 1 x pair of boots
- [ ] 1 x knife
- [ ] 1 x compound hunting bow
- [ ] 1 x cooker (I always carry a solid-fuel burner for trips over 15 days)
- [ ] 2 x GoPro Hero5 cameras and 1 x GoPro Hero Session camera, so I could film my adventure
- [ ] 3 x battery packs to run my cameras, satellite phone and cellphone
- [ ] 3 x solar panels for charging the battery packs
- [ ] 2 x solar torches

- [ ] 1 x satellite phone
- [ ] 1 x personal locator beacon
- [ ] 1 x survival kit (mine is huge — I use it almost every day, it's more of a life kit; it has string, a flint, a candle, fishing hooks, a scalpel and that kind of stuff)
- [ ] 1 x first aid kit
- [ ] 1 x pen and notebook
- [ ] 1 x pot
- [ ] 1 x pan
- [ ] 1 x spoon (you can do pretty much everything with a spoon!)
- [ ] Dry bags for everything (that means a dry bag for wet stuff, too)
- [ ] 1 x inflatable roll mat (if you're going to take luxuries, make sure they're for sleeping or eating!)
- [ ] 1 x sleeping bag and thermal liner
- [ ] 1 x survival bivvy bag

✗

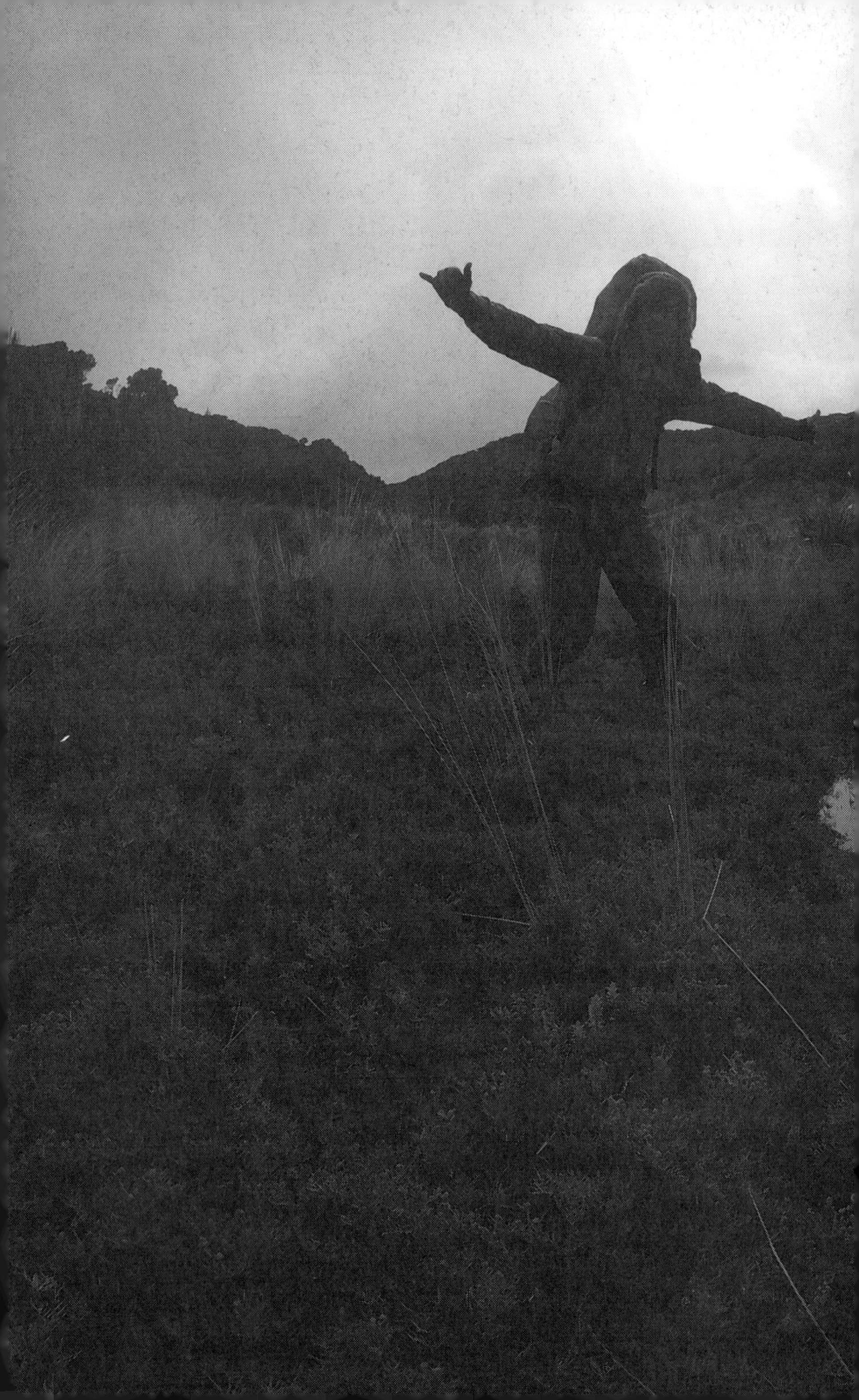

Chapter Three
INTO THE UNKNOWN

Day 1
10.11.16
Oban to Bungaree Hut
19 km

Anyone who has ever shared a room with me will tell you that I'm not the tidiest of people. As soon as I get into a room, stuff from my pack seems to find its way all over the place. My room at the backpackers was no different. Before I could get moving on my first day, I had to gather up all my stuff and repack my bags. This morning, it was slower than usual as I had to make doubly sure I had everything I needed — I didn't know when I'd be back.

OWING TO THE FACT that my plans were a bit flexible, and I didn't know quite how long I'd be gone for, I had to carry as much as I could. As a result, my pack was very full and very heavy. Once I'd got all my gear ready, everything suddenly felt real. I was suddenly very nervous. I stood there looking in the mirror, saying to myself, 'You can do this. You can do whatever you want to do with your life. You can achieve the impossible. Believe in yourself.'

I don't know if I really believed any of it, though. The truth is I was nervous and I didn't know if I could do it — not just because of how hard it was going to be physically, but because I knew how much I was going to miss my Wildgirl.

Before I could start the day's walk, I had to go to the DOC office to pick up my last permit. Then I stopped at a café and had a massive-as breakfast: bacon, eggs, sausages, hash browns, tomatoes and toast. It would be the last proper meal I would have for a while and it was so, so good.

After breakfast, I went to Halfmoon Bay School to talk to the kids there. That was heaps of fun. It's an awesome little school with only about 30 kids. Their motto is 'A choppy sea can be navigated'. I like that. The kids were really cool — they have such a great life. I was super impressed by the amount of outdoor stuff they do at the school — they even have a thing called Bush School for the little kids, where they study science in the outdoors. I wish they'd had that when I was at school.

We went down to the beach in front of the school. This was the moment I had been waiting for, the beginning of the journey. I got all the kids to step over the line I'd drawn in the sand. They were stoked to be a part of my adventure. We all set off together, and the kids showed me the secret locals' track around to the bathing beach at the northern end of the bay. I walked but most of them ran.

The kids were so excited to be outside on a school day, exploring around the rocks. I felt so proud that I had started this.

They were having so much fun and had so many questions for me. The kids walked with me around to

Horseshoe Bay, before they had to go back to school. We had a massive group hug and they headed back, all laughing and talking. Then I was on my own. Having the kids with me had made me feel excited, but the nervousness was still there.

After Horseshoe Bay, I walked around the coast for a bit. But it was rocky and rugged, and I'd underestimated just how difficult it would be to get around with my 30-kilogram pack on. I got about 100 metres and was like 'This is impossible!'

I came to a clay cliff that climbed straight up out of the sea. It was about 30 metres up to the top of the cliff, so I decided to climb up it. It was terrifying. It was really steep and covered in rocks and fallen branches. The ground was so loose and almost everything I grabbed was loose, too. I thought I was going to fall at any moment.

Just before I got up to the top I slipped, and a stick punctured my right hand. It hurt, but I pulled out the stick, chucked some sand in the hole to try to stop the bleeding and climbed the rest of the way up the cliff.

At the top I used my first aid kit to deal with my wound. Fortunately, it wasn't as bad as I had originally thought — it just bled a lot.

Once I'd fixed myself up, I carried on walking along the edge of a predator-proof fence that runs along the edge of the privately owned 172-hectare Dancing Star Estate eco-sanctuary. The fence runs between Horseshoe Bay and Lee Bay, pretty much cutting off access to the Mamaku Point headland. It would be the last bit of privately owned land that I would see for a while, as Lee

Bay marks the entrance to Rakiura National Park. It's the newest of New Zealand's national parks, having been set up in 2002, and like I've said, it covers about 85 per cent of the island.

There was a firebreak in the bush next to the fence, so walking was very easy but at times it got steep and slippery. There were birds everywhere, even birds I had never heard before.

I saw my first white-tail deer on this bit of my adventure, too. I came up over the brow of one of the hills and right there in front of me was a young deer. I dropped down to the ground, took my bow and slowly started crawling towards the creature.

When I was about 10 metres away, I strung an arrow and slowly rose from the long grass to take aim. As I did, the deer looked straight into my eyes. His eyes were big and black and it felt like I was looking into its soul as I looked down the shaft of my arrow. I realised I couldn't bring myself to kill this animal, especially when I wasn't desperate for food. It was so beautiful and it would have been a waste of a life.

I lowered my bow and slowly sat back down in the grass. The deer approached to get a better look at me. It got so close I could have almost touched it.

That moment was so incredible. I was so confused. I had never been approached by a wild deer like that before. It made me realise that since I had finished my walk around New Zealand, I had grown as a human being in such a positive way but I had lost the deep connection that I'd had with nature. That made me feel sad.

I followed the fence until it popped out at Lee Bay. The bay is also the start of the Rakiura Track, which is one of New Zealand's nine Great Walks. The walks are all managed by DOC and they're popular with both Kiwis and people from overseas. The Rakiura Track is a 32-kilometre loop that most walkers take about three days to cover. I planned to follow the track for the first day, as far as Port William hut, then head off on the North West Circuit track.

The entrance to the park is marked by a chain-link sculpture. It was built to symbolise Maui using Rakiura as an anchor to keep the South Island — his waka — in place. The other end of the chain sculpture is near Stirling Point, just out of Bluff, on the mainland.

The first few kilometres were cruisy — the track is really well maintained. In fact, it almost looks like a road — all gravelled and groomed, and with the trees trimmed! It meant that I could go quite fast but it also meant I didn't really feel like I was having an adventure. However, it gave me plenty of time to check out the scenery, which was beautiful. The beaches were golden, the water was an intense turquoise-blue, the sun was shining and there were huge tree ferns overhead. If you saw a photo you'd think that it was a tropical paradise. Except for one thing — it was cold!

Because I didn't have to be super focused on where I was going, I spent a bit of time collecting the fresh shoots off supplejack vines. They are full of moisture and taste a bit like asparagus or green beans — my first bush food of the trip and they were delicious.

That first day, I noticed just how amazing the air smelled. The native bush has this crisp, clean smell that I absolutely love. I'd forgotten how good that smell is. I quickly realised that finding fresh water wouldn't be a problem at all. There were creeks, streams, rivers and little waterfalls all over the place. That was a relief, as it was one less thing for me to worry about.

The rivers on the island have heaps of tannin in them, so the water was really brown. When leaves and other plant matter rot on the floor of the forest, they release tannins that then get washed into the water. It's perfectly natural and gives the water a quite earthy taste. Even though it was a weird shade of brown, the water was so fresh and delicious.

The rata trees I was walking through were absolute giants, and it felt as though the whole place was completely untouched.

The other thing I noticed was that there were so many rats — a ridiculous number. I counted about 47 rats between the start and Port William. In the end I gave up counting. There were hundreds of them everywhere, just cruising around in the middle of the day. I later found out that because the weather had been so good over the past year, there was a huge amount of rimu seeds for them to eat (that's one of their primary foods), so the population had boomed. Apparently, the seeds were running out though and they had started to eat each other. Cannibal rats!

Rakiura National Park

The fourteenth national park in New Zealand, Rakiura was opened in 2002. Before that, the island's conservation land was made up of a complicated mixture of scenic reserves and state forest areas. It's hard to imagine now that anyone would have wanted to cut down the amazing ancient trees I saw on the island. There are massive old rimu, totara and kahikatea trees by the dozen.

The park makes up about 85 per cent of Stewart Island's land area, covering 1570 square kilometres of land, making it New Zealand's third largest national park after Fiordland and Kahurangi.

The land that isn't part of the national park is mostly around Halfmoon Bay. There's also a bit of land on the eastern side of the island that's managed by the Rakiura Maori Land Trust.

Because of its isolation, the park is home to all sorts of awesome native birds, many of which I was lucky enough to see while I was there. Most people know about the kakapo on the offshore islands near Stewart Island, but there are also heaps of their parrot cousins, the kaka and the kakariki, as well as tui, bellbirds, Stewart Island robins, dotterels, yellow-eyed penguins, weka and heaps of other cool birds.

Stewart Island also has its own special kiwi population. The southern tokoeka (or Rakiura kiwi) are different from

The beaches were golden, the water was an intense turquoise-blue, the sun was shining . . . If you saw a photo you'd think that it was a tropical paradise. Except for one thing — it was cold!

I had five, I climbed out of the icy water and dried off. My skin felt like it had shrunk to my body I was so cold.

It was a sunny day, and the sun had been heating the rocks all my clothes were on. It was a nice feeling putting on warm clothes. I took the paua meat out of the shells and put it in a dry bag for later.

I followed the coast around the corner from my dive spot, then climbed up into the bush to where I knew the track would be. As I walked towards my campsite for the night, the clouds made unique shapes in the sky and I created scenes in my head with them.

By about 5.15 p.m. on that first day, my back started to really give me a hard time. It had been about a year since my back surgery and until that day it hadn't caused me any problems. To be fair, I hadn't carried so much weight on my back over that time, but now it really hurt. This wasn't good — especially as this was only my first day.

✕

Types of fun

American climber Kelly Cordes reckons he first heard about the fun scale from an adventurer called Peter Haeussler in 2001. On his website (www.kellycordes.com) he describes the three types of fun.

I like this idea, so have put together my own Wildboy fun scale.

Type one fun: It's real fun. You're having a good time 99 per cent of the time you are doing the activity. Like kayaking on a beautiful day or having a drink with some mates.

Type two fun: It's not fun at the time. It's a challenge and you often need to dig deep to push through. But when you're finished, you look back and think about how much fun it was, like ice climbing or hiking in a storm.

Type three fun: It's a fun idea in your head, but in reality it's horrid and you find yourself thinking 'What the heck am I doing?' When you make it to the end, you're nothing but glad that it's over, like eating the world's hottest chillies.

×

AS THE EVENING WORE ON, my mental state gradually got worse. Doubts echoed around my head, my back screamed in pain and my lungs burned as I climbed between bays. Eventually, the tears came. I was having total type-two fun. All I could do was try to convince myself that I'd look back on this and think it had been worth it. It was day one, and I was already losing my mind.

Looking back, I've realised just how disconnected from nature I'd become since I finished my trip around New Zealand. On this trip I had to learn how to reconnect, and nature was not going to make it easy for me.

I eventually arrived at a DOC campsite, where I contemplated camping. I had walked about 17 kilometres and I was tired — but there was a fire burning inside me that was driving me to continue. I carried on another couple of kilometres until I got to Bungaree Hut. It was a huge day — I had walked about 19 kilometres in about six hours. There were a whole lot of DOC workers at the hut who all knew each other and I felt a bit weird going in and joining them, so I set up my tent outside. I didn't want to tell people that I was walking around Stewart Island when I'd only been going for one day.

I got out my paua and some supplejack I had picked for dinner. My liquid gas cooker wouldn't even start. The gas that I brought wouldn't work — I think I had the wrong fuel — so dinner was going to be cold. I was gutted! Raw paua is almost inedible because of its rubbery texture. That messed me up, because the thing I had been looking forward to was having a hot meal — and I couldn't get one.

Just when I had given up on cooking dinner, a friendly man came out of the hut and offered me his gas cooker. I was so thankful that I was going to get my hot meal, and it was flippin' delish!

I was a bit worried about how I'd cope without a cooker but I figured that if I could ask Dad to see if he could get some fuel brought into Mason Bay then it would only be five days of cold food. If I couldn't get fuel there, then I was facing the whole trip without a burner and that worried me a bit.

My body was exhausted from such a big day. I had been physically and emotionally challenged and, at times, I had really struggled. I had times where I thought that going into this big adventure had been a silly idea.

Lying in my tent, I began to think about Ngaio and how much I missed her. It was just becoming apparent that this was going to be a very lonely adventure, and it scared me. I sat outside and watched the stars move as the earth turned before sliding into my tent to get some much-needed rest.

> Day 2
> 11.11.16
> Bungaree Hut to Christmas Village Hut
> 11.5 km

MY DIARY FOR THE second day of my trip started with these three lines:

Very hard day
SO hungry!!!
Body hates me

I THINK THAT PRETTY much summed up the day. I set off at about 9 a.m. and the bush was amazing. It was so noisy. The birds make quite a racket, singing happily, and there's this low buzz of insects. The only other noises were the sound of my footsteps, my breath when the going got a bit tough and — to amuse myself — me whistling at the birds. They didn't whistle back, which was a bit disappointing.

The first day's mud was tame compared to today's — it reached easily halfway up my calves and was very sloshy.

The difference between the Rakiura Track, which is well groomed all year round, and the North West Circuit, which gets much less attention, became more obvious the further I walked. The track isn't really a track — it's a route. As well as the mud, there were a lot of tree roots to navigate and the odd sand dune to climb, which made for slow going.

By 10 a.m., I'd been walking for an hour. My state of mind hadn't improved much overnight so I was feeling pretty miserable. Being hungry probably didn't help — I had decided to try to save as much of the food I was carrying in case I needed it later in the trip, so I hadn't eaten anything that morning. I was so hungry that I sat down and had one of my freeze-dried meals cold. I just opened the packet, tipped in cold water and let it reconstitute. Having something to eat definitely made me feel a bit better.

My plan had been to do about 20 kilometres and camp out in the bush. But I changed my plan and decided to head to Christmas Village Bay, which was only about 11 kilometres from Bungaree.

The beaches along the coast here were something else. They were so beautiful. The sand was golden, and there was something special about mine being the only footprints on them. The sand was edged by native grasses, which then gave way to podocarp and hardwood forests. The track wound through open forest, the trees reaching high above the low-growing ferns. There was no dense, low undergrowth like you see in the North Island — it was all just open and light.

There were plenty of fern-lined creeks along the way

where I could stop and drink fresh, cool water. Like the first day, most of the water was a bit brown, but it tasted delicious. The forest was all so untouched. This is how New Zealand must have looked before people arrived.

Water

Water wasn't ever a problem — beautiful fresh water was everywhere. There were so many creeks and rivers that weren't even on the map. If they marked every single creek on the map the whole thing would just be blue! There's nothing to pollute the water so I didn't have to worry about drinking it ever.

IT WAS ONLY DAY TWO and I was already starting to obsess about food. I made a note that the first thing I was going to eat when I got out was a whole tub of ice cream. I was so hungry all day, even having eaten one of my meals. It became clear really early on that I hadn't really thought through the whole food situation, and I was going to have to do something about it if I was going to make it through this adventure. I realised that on my trip around New Zealand, a lot of people gave me food along the way. There weren't going to be a lot of people here so that probably wasn't going to happen. I hadn't really factored in the temperature of the water down here either, so getting seafood wasn't going to be as easy as I thought.

I don't think I've ever been so happy to see a sign as I was when I finally got to a DOC post pointing towards Christmas Village Hut. Once I knew a bed was only five minutes away, I made up my mind — I was staying in that bad boy for the night. I just didn't have another 8 kilometres in me for the day.

Christmas Village Bay was different from the other beaches I'd been on that day. It was covered in big, smooth rocks, with the bush coming down to the edge of the sand. Buzzing above the rocks was my welcoming committee — a whole lot of seriously massive sandflies. There were so many of them it was ridiculous.

I met this really cool guy, Ant, in the hut, which was just above the beach. He knew a lot about the wilderness way of life. That's how he lives: he works, then goes off into the bush and chills out, works, goes off into the bush and chills out some more. He had spent quite a bit of time on the island and gave me some good advice. He even knew which spots on the track I'd be able to get cellphone coverage!

Physically, it was quite a tough day and the bloody sandflies were killing me. My back and shoulders were incredibly sore. I'm not sure if there were marks on my shoulders from my pack, but they felt pretty bruised. But I definitely felt better than I had the day before. My emotions were still all over the show, too — self-doubt was consuming me and I figured it might take a few more days before I really got into the swing of things.

I was challenged by the lack of food, so I was stoked to get some more paua. I went out diving just off Christmas Village Bay. The water was fairly flat so getting the paua was straightforward. I also tried to catch a fish, without any luck.

There were still heaps of rats everywhere — but nowhere near as many as there were sandflies. The insects are insane here — huge and very persistent.

Ant was staying at the hut that night as well, so we spent quite a bit of time sitting at the table talking. He shared some food with me, and I discovered just how good dates taste when they're covered in peanut butter. Good company and a belly full of food made me feel much better when I went to bed that night.

Day 3
12.11.16
Christmas Village Hut to Yankee River Hut
12 km

I SLEPT SO WELL at Christmas Village Hut, but my body was really sore when I got up. The most painful parts were my hips and my shoulders — there was some quite gnarly bruising where my pack had been sitting.

Just as I was about to leave the hut, it started to rain. I hoped it wouldn't stick around too long, but I figured that if it did, it was just another part of the adventure. I estimated that my walk for the day would take about six hours, and I knew that there were a couple of steep climbs on the track.

As I walked, I noticed that the birdlife was getting even more prolific; despite all the rats, there were birds everywhere. The bush was much denser, too, with much larger trees just about everywhere — and I'm talking seriously tall rata trees that almost hurt my neck to look up at them. That got me thinking about the fact that a lot of the time people forget to look up. Sometimes what we need is right in front of us — or in my case that day, right above me! Once I started really taking in my surroundings and admiring the beauty of the forest, I actually began to enjoy myself a bit.

I couldn't stop thinking about food all day. I had decided to set out with no breakfast again so I could save my food for later in the trip. Silly mistake! I came across some fallen logs with a bunch of holes in them, so I got my knife out and hacked into the wood, hoping to find some big, fat huhu grubs. Unfortunately, they weren't home.

One thing I did discover was that my Absolute Wilderness food pouches made excellent water holders. I'd rinse them out once I'd finished the meal, fill them with water and carry them for drinking water during the day. It was so much easier than mucking around with the hydration pouch I had in my backpack. I could just dip these little pouches into a stream or river and fill them really easily without mucking around taking off my pack.

The mud was terrible again — it came up higher than my boots and was sloshy and wet. It would occur in random patches along the track and they varied in size and depth massively. But I discovered one good thing about all the mud, too. In the middle of one big muddy patch I was super stoked to find my first kiwi footprint. Now I just had to find the kiwi!

The track was also littered with gnarly, slippery roots. At one point, I took quite a big fall and my arm got caught on a branch. It felt like it just about ripped out of the socket.

Because the rain had stopped and the sun was shining, I got out my solar panels to charge some stuff. I opened them up and attached them to the top of my pack while I was walking. I had three of them, so one could be charging my phone, one charging another battery and the other one in reserve. I also had a couple of little solar-powered torches that clipped onto the front strap of my pack. Pretty cool technology just using the sun, I reckon.

Most of the day was a mixture of following the track and making my way around the coast, which meant

Looking back, I've realised just how disconnected from nature I'd become since I finished my trip around New Zealand. On this trip I had to learn how to reconnect, and nature was not going to make it easy for me.

walking along sandy beaches, but more often meant clambering over rocks. I could tell I was getting nearer the western side of the island, as the coast was becoming a little more rugged.

At one point, I found a spot where I had cellphone coverage and managed to make a couple of calls. The whole time I was being buzzed by sandflies, which was annoying. I had a long talk to my dad, who said he was going to try to source me a new cooker and some staple food. I was frothing at the thought of having both of those things waiting for me at Mason Bay. I was due to arrive there in four days' time.

I'd realised quite quickly that my 30 meals weren't going to be enough, and I hadn't had that much luck catching food. I'd pretty much been eating paua for the past two days so the idea of having some rice and some flour to cook with was epic.

I found carrying my pack hard going again. What looked like little hills would completely smash me with my pack on. Total destruction. My back was killing me and I was scared I wouldn't be able to complete the trip because of it. I thought a lot about what I could get rid of to lighten my pack, and decided I was going to leave my hunting bow at Mason Bay. It was so heavy and a pain to carry and also, I really didn't want to shoot deer. I knew that if I did it, I'd end up wasting meat because there was only so much I could eat or carry, and that felt really wrong to me. I couldn't wait until I was back into prime walking fitness, but there was only one way that would happen, and that was to keep on walking.

As the day wore on, my brain started to get away on me again. I was thinking too much about the past — things I'd done and things I should have done. It wasn't good for me. At one point, I had a full emotional breakdown. I burst into tears and was just yelling at the sky. After being so excited about the trip for so long, I struggled with feeling like I didn't want to be here, and that I didn't want to be doing this. I couldn't work out what was making me feel this way — partly it was the lack of food, but I'd never felt that way about an adventure before.

The more I thought about it, the lonelier I felt. I kept thinking about what everyone would be doing back home. I had had so much fun over the past year hanging out with a cool bunch of people in Nelson, and suddenly here I was in a beautiful place — on my own.

This was my time off from uni and I could have been spending it with my girlfriend. Ngaio and I had been living apart for a year and I felt like a really bad boyfriend. The time I could have been enjoying with her, I was at the other end of the country having an adventure.

I felt like I'd ruined my life by walking around New Zealand, which isn't true. I felt like that was defining who I was and I didn't want it to. I was starving. I wasn't happy. I just wanted to go home. Looking back now, I realise that I just hadn't been eating enough and my mind wasn't working properly. Instead of thinking 'I should eat more', I was thinking 'I should have weaned myself off food before I came down here'. I had been eating huge meals all year, and the days before setting off I was eating, eating, eating. I'd had a huge breakfast the day I left and then, boom, nothing. The odd freeze-dried meal, some paua and a bit of supplejack and that was it.

Eventually, I decided that I'd become completely disconnected from the real, natural world. Social media had taken control of my life; I was focusing on some of the wrong stuff in my day-to-day. I didn't realise how lost I'd become. At one point, I had even written in my diary 'the wild needs me'. The truth was that *I* needed the wild. I needed that connection with the wilderness once more. I had to learn to reconnect with nature.

I stopped on a little beach and completely lost control of my emotions. I was tired, irritable and hungry. I already wanted to give up. I wanted to go home. As the tears flowed from my face, I felt lost. I decided I had to do something about it, rather than just going round and round in my head, so I drew another line in the sand. On one side was the past and everything in it — on the other was the present. Once I stepped over the line, I would be in the present and I needed to try to stay there for the rest of the trip. Taking that step made me feel way better than I thought it would!

Another thing that made me feel pretty good was coming across another one of those yellow and green DOC signs. This one said 'Long Harry Hut 4.5 hours'. Then, next to an arrow pointing in the opposite direction, were the words 'Yankee River Hut 10 minutes'. No prizes for guessing where I was going.

I turned and headed down the hill towards Yankee River, and about five minutes later arrived at the hut. It was a fairly standard-looking DOC hut — painted green with a large verandah on the front — but it was sitting right on the banks of a little river.

I followed a small track down to the mouth of the river. It was rocky but I managed to climb down to the water's edge. I was just carrying a handline, which is a pretty simple reel, but I caught my first fish — yes! Then I decided to chop it up and use it for bait so I could catch an even bigger fish. Unfortunately, there was no bigger fish. I was so annoyed!

I collected some king-sized limpets off the rocks — they were almost the size of paua — and took them back to the hut for dinner. I also went for a dive and got some paua but decided I'd hang onto them for tomorrow, given there was plenty of protein around today. I always like to do a bit of forward planning, just in case.

✕

Edible plants

You might be surprised at some of the things that you can eat while you're out in the wild. I ate a bit of supplejack while I was on Stewart Island, but there are quite a few other common plants that you can add to your diet when you're out having adventures (just not while you're in national parks, as that's not allowed).

For example, you can eat the youngest shoot in the middle of a cabbage tree. One of my favourites is the sweet orange pollen on flax flowers. Fiddlehead ferns are another popular one — they're also known as pikopiko and they taste a bit like asparagus. There are also several edible seaweed species that can be added to your diet.

The most important thing about eating wild plants is to be sure that what you're eating isn't poisonous. When I did my walk around New Zealand, one of the things I carried with me the whole way was Andrew Crowe's book *A Field Guide to the Native Edible Plants of New Zealand*. I used it to make sure that the plants I was eating were safe, and it also gave me some ideas of things to eat that I wouldn't have thought of.

×

> Day 4
> 13.11.16
> Yankee River Hut to Long Harry Hut
> 9 km

ON THE MORNING OF my fourth day, I decided to slow down a little bit because I was struggling to make the progress I wanted to on the food that I had. I adjusted my plan for the day and decided to walk the 9 kilometres to Long Harry Hut instead of trying to go further and camp.

Before I set out, I had a freeze-dried meal for breakfast — pasta in a Bolognaise sauce. I heated some water on the pot-belly stove in the hut and mixed it all up. It was so good to have a hot meal and it made a real difference to my energy levels during the day.

The day started with a 200-metre climb up a really muddy ridge. The climbs were still quite hard on my legs with the big heavy pack but I felt like my fitness was coming back. The other side was just as steep but it went down into the most amazing sand dunes. There were kiwi footprints everywhere. I crossed a small river at the end of the beach and then climbed steeply back up into the bush.

The open forest turned a bit more scrubby as I made my way around the coast. Starting to see the scrub got me thinking about what I was going to see as I got closer to the south coast. Even here, it looked almost impenetrable. That made me nervous. I'd get frights quite a bit — there would be a little tiny cracking sound in the bush and I'd spin around to see what caused it. It was a sound I'd never heard in the bush before, and each time I heard it, I thought it might be a person. And each time I'd turn around, I'd see rats. Heaps and heaps of rats. That took a bit of getting used to.

Every now and then the forest would open out into the most beautiful views. Then there was a little gap in the bush and through it I saw a sweep of golden beach and this blue, blue water. It looked so good I stopped in my tracks and remembered why I was doing this.

The high of seeing the beach soon disappeared when the track took me through a creek and straight up a massive sand dune. It didn't take long before my lungs started to scream and I was struggling. Walking up sand is hard work, never mind doing it into a head wind with a massive pack on. Going down the other side and onto

Smoky Beach was much more fun! The beach was about a kilometre long and right at the end of it I could see the headland that Long Harry Hut — my stop for the night — was on. It was going to take a bit of a climb to get to the hut but at least I could see where I was heading.

The day definitely went better than the previous one. I think having breakfast made me feel much better. I knew I had paua for dinner but wasn't looking forward to just eating plain paua.

The hut was perched up on the headland, with a great view over the sea. It was empty when I got there so I made myself at home. There were a couple of sets of bunks, a big table with benches around it, a pot-belly stove, a map on the wall and a big stainless-steel sink-bench inside the hut, all of which is pretty much standard for a DOC hut on the island.

There was also a stainless-steel sink outside, so I made the most of the opportunity and washed my clothes in it. The colour of the water once my socks and shirt had been in there was so disgusting! I hung my washing to dry on a line on the edge of the verandah and let the wind do its thing. I was so looking forward to having clean, dry gear to put on.

Back inside I set up my three solar panels and my two solar torches on the windowsill to charge. It was so good to see the sun and blue sky. I just hoped that it would stay that way for a bit longer.

With my batteries charging, I called Dad. He told me that he'd managed to source a BioLite stove for me. They're these brilliant wood burners that you can cook on and charge batteries off. He said he'd see if there was anyone in Oban who might be able to bring it over to Mason Bay Hut before I got there. I so hoped he'd be able to, because then I wouldn't need to carry fuel with me and I wouldn't have to worry about not having enough sun to charge my batteries. I knew that I'd be going out of cellphone coverage the next day, so I wouldn't know if he'd managed to get it in until I got to Mason Bay.

Having arrived at the hut kind of early in the day, I headed out to try to get myself some dinner. I walked down the hill to the beach, stripped off and went into the sea. Once again, it was so unbelievably cold in the water that I couldn't stay in for long but I managed to get some more paua — but this time it was yellow-foot — and a couple of kina. I'd been eating black-foot so finding yellow-foot was exciting. It tasted the same but it was new to me! It's slightly smaller and a different colour but that's all really.

Back at the hut, I devised a cunning plan to get warm and clean. All of the huts have big old metal buckets to put the ash from the fire in. I cleaned out the ash bucket, filled it up with water and put it on top of the stove. Twenty minutes later, I had enough water for me to have a hot bath. Well, kind of. I stripped off, went outside on the verandah and tipped pans of hot water over myself as I watched the sun setting. Could this day get any better? Well, yes, it turned out it could.

With clean clothes, food and a hot bath, I was feeling so much better. My dinner got me freaking frothing. After being so unhappy about having plain paua, I managed to cook up a storm. Did you know that if you slice black-foot paua thin and fry it for long enough it tastes a bit like crispy cheese? I love cheese. That meal was the best paua I've eaten in my whole life — a bit of soy sauce, a bit of pepper, a pinch of salt and I was very happy.

Then I decided to try cooking some yellow-foot paua, but this time a different way. And who would have thought paua could taste like bacon? It was delicious. Here's the recipe: get your paua, slice it up, put it in a pan with some canola oil, which I found at the hut, then put it inside the pot-belly stove and roast it so that it's all smoky and goes crispy and delicious around the edges and still a bit chewy in the middle. Oh my god — so good! I felt like I was almost back to my old self.

After having been so down in the dumps the previous day, I felt way better. I was still a bit confused about how I had got to be so unhappy with myself but also had plenty of time to think about that over the coming days. I still missed my girlfriend a lot but so far I'd been able to talk to her pretty much whenever I wanted. Going out of cell coverage was going to change that, and I knew I was going to miss her even more.

✕

Rats!

One of the things that shocked me about the island was just how many rats there were — they were everywhere!

I did my best to kill a few but that wouldn't have made much difference to the population.

The main thing that the rats feed on is flowers and fruit from the rimu tree. Some years the trees produce an abundance of seeds — these are called mast years. There had been two mast years in a row when I was on Stewart Island so rat numbers had gone ballistic — the more food they have, the more they can breed.

Then, when there isn't enough food, they start eating birds and eggs. The good news is that kiwi have been filmed fighting off rats, and kiwi eggs are too big to fit in a rat's mouth. The bad news is kiwi are just one of heaps of different bird breeds on the island. The tiny Stewart Island robin wouldn't be difficult for a rat to take out.

The locals are doing their best to work out what to do about the rat infestation, and this is being driven by a group called Predator Free Stewart Island. They work with DOC and some other organisations with the goal of eliminating all predators (except pet cats and dogs) from the island. At the moment, DOC are focusing on getting rid of feral cats, which are a threat to the southern New Zealand dotterel and the harlequin gecko, as well as other bird species.

✕

> Day 5
> 14.11.16
> Long Harry Hut to East Ruggedy Hut
> 9.5 km

I'D HAD A DECENT SLEEP but I woke up to a whole heap of messages on my cellphone. I thought it was a bit weird to get so many, so I was a bit worried that something bad had happened. Something had happened all right — there had been a huge earthquake near Kaikoura and there had been tsunami warnings all along the coast of the South Island. I hadn't felt anything and I had no idea about the possible tsunami as I'd been fast asleep. I woke up to get all these messages from people saying 'Tsunami warning! Get away from the coast!' It was nice to know people were thinking of me. I got told that there was heaps of damage further north, but I soon worked out that everyone I knew was OK.

Even after my delicious dinner, I was pretty hungry again and there was no breakfast. In hindsight, walking all that distance every day and not eating was not smart. I think that's why I was so miserable. Rationing my food was really tough on my brain. I could push my body through these things fine but my brain was just fizzling out. I was angry, I was upset — it wasn't good.

I left the hut at 10 a.m., headed for East Ruggedy Hut, which was about 10 kilometres away. Despite the hunger, my body was beginning to cope better. I felt like the walking was becoming more manageable and I was more in tune with my environment. That made me feel a bit more like I would cope with tackling the south coast.

I did worry a bit that my adventure would be over just as my body came right, though.

Quite early on in the day I got a bit emotional while I was walking through a bit of bush where the light shone on young manuka trees just like at a ranch where my girlfriend and I rode horses together in the Coromandel. Even though it had only been five days, I'd be spending a lot longer than that away from her. Thinking about Ngaio made me realise how much I love her, and that I spend way too much time worrying about the future and not enough time living in the now.

When I set off on the journey, I didn't think it would be as emotional as it was. It only took five days before I understood that the trip was going to provide me with the dramatic change in my life that I needed. Up until then, I'd felt like it was all about proving what an adventurer I was, about ticking off another mission. But it wasn't about those things at all. It was about making some changes in me and in my life.

It made me appreciate that I'd lost the connection I'd had with what I loved most: the wilderness. Social media had influenced how I lived my life. I was doing a lot of things to make other people happy and to fulfil other people's expectations, instead of just doing what I loved. I felt huge pressure to be doing things and then posting about them to keep other people entertained, instead of doing stuff because I wanted to. Being out of cell coverage meant that I missed talking to my family and my girlfriend, but it was really nice to not have to post stuff just for the sake of it.

MY WANDERING BRAIN WAS quickly brought back to the present when I saw movement low down on the trail ahead of me. It was 11.30 a.m. and the sun was out so I did a bit of a double take — it was a big kiwi snuffling around in the leaves. I stood very still and just watched it, barely breathing, as I didn't want to scare it away. It turned towards me, walked up the track in my direction a little bit then happily wandered off into the undergrowth.

I was so emotional. I burst into tears. I'd heard about these birds since before I can remember. I'd been out and tracked kiwi with rangers in the North Island before, which was cool, but to see one in its natural environment, in the middle of the day, just chilling out, walking in front of me was incredible. I could barely believe it. It's hard to explain how I felt after that — incredibly lucky and just a whole lot happier. My first Stewart Island kiwi! It almost didn't seem real. It gave me a real burst of energy to keep walking.

As well as the kiwi, rats kept me company along the way. It's a bit weird but because they don't really see a lot of people, they're not that scared of humans.

Walking away from Long Harry Hut, I knew that today was the day when I would walk around the north of the island and onto its wild west coast. From walking through big, ancient native forest I found myself stepping through manuka scrub. It was really windswept and all the bush was flat on top. It was quite dark underneath it, so there wasn't much in the way of groundcover.

The track pretty much stuck to the cliffs around the

coast so the views were spectacular. When it did go down to the water, the drops were really steep, covered in scrub. The beaches were now far more rocky — actually, they were bouldery — and there wasn't much sand to be seen. It took a bit of rock hopping to get along the beaches, and at some points the big rocks were hard to climb over. Even though it was quite a calm day, the sea was much wilder than on the north coast and I could tell that from now on getting paua could be difficult.

After about four hours, the excitement of the kiwi had worn off and my whole body felt wrecked. I felt like I needed two days' rest and a heap of food, but I couldn't see how any of that would happen in the next few days.

A few minutes later, I dropped my pack to go and check out a lookout. The track took me through a tangle of roots and vines and then climbed high up to a bluff. As I was walking along, as if by magic, I saw another kiwi. This one was in the middle of a clump of tussocky grass under some trees — I think it's called turpentine bush because it smells of turps. It was so close I could have touched it (but I didn't — obviously!). It had a good look at me then scooted off into the undergrowth — but it gave me another burst of energy to keep going. I couldn't believe my luck.

The lookout itself was amazing, too. From up there I could see down to East Ruggedy Beach, and beyond it the sweep of the west coast and out to Codfish Island/Whenua Hou. It was beautiful and scary at the same time. While I was up there it started to rain so I was glad to know that East Ruggedy Hut wasn't too far away.

Heading down the hill from the lookout, I ended up in some head-high manuka scrub. It was quite open and I managed to push my way through it quite easily. I decided that if that was what the scrub was like on the south coast, I'd be absolutely fine.

At East Ruggedy Beach there is a big sandy basin where the Ruggedy Stream meets the sea. It's a wild-looking place, with loads of driftwood all over the place. The sandy basin and the dunes around it were flecked with pingao, which gave it this strange orange colour.

At one point, I was crossing the stream when I dropped right up to my hip in soft sand. The water was suddenly up to my shoulders. It was terrifying. Every time I moved I went a little bit deeper. Quicksand was something I'd been warned about on the island, so I began to panic when I started to sink. Luckily, I had only one foot in it and I could drag myself out. It was absolutely terrifying, though.

To get to the hut, I had to walk through the dunes, back into the bush and a short way up the stream. I still wasn't sure whether I'd stop there or carry on further to the campsite on West Ruggedy Beach, but I figured I'd check the place out anyway.

I was so happy that I did! In the hut, I found a bucket under the bench. It wasn't just any bucket, though. In the bucket was *food*. People would just leave behind stuff that they didn't need. There was salt, pepper, oil, rice, milk powder, flour and, best of all, potato flakes! There was also a cooler hanging outside, which I went and checked out. In it was some butter. Quite a bit of it had been eaten by rats but I didn't care — I cut off the bad bits and used it anyway. I love milk powder, it's one of my favourite things. I made little shots of super-creamy milk and just ate it off a spoon.

There was no question in my mind — I was staying in the hut tonight and I was going to eat like a king. For dinner, I decided to have paua cooked in butter. *Yeah! That's what I'm talking about!*

I made a mixture of flour, salt, pepper and a bit of milk powder — all of which came from the free food bucket. I was going to have battered paua for dinner! I shallow-fried it in some rice bran oil that was in the bucket, too. Then I ate it with mashed potato made from the flakes. Delicious.

I made some damper as well, so I had something to eat while I was walking the next day. It's basically just flour and water, fried in the fire with a bit of oil. I also chucked some butter in so it was a real fatty, tasty treat. That epic meal certainly made up for having started the day with no food.

The hut was bloody beautiful, with a view out into the bush. I was lucky to be able to stay in huts for the first bit of the expedition. I had the place to myself, so I got the fire going quickly. It had started raining heavily so I was happy to be inside and warm.

I was full and happy, but there would be challenges ahead of me the next day. It had started raining and from what I'd heard, when it starts raining on Stewart Island, it doesn't stop. If it didn't stop, the challenge for the next few days would be mud. The mud that was already there would turn into slushy mud, and that would not be fun.

The water was suddenly up to my shoulders. It was terrifying. Every time I moved I went a little bit deeper. Quicksand was something I'd been warned about on the island, so I began to panic when I started to sink.

At the end of the night, my final words in my diary for the day were:

It's pretty hard to tell how I'm feeling. I miss my girlfriend, I miss my family. But I know I can do this. But not without food. As long as I can keep fed, I'll be sweet.

Quicksand

So many movies feature baddies sitting by while the hero sinks in quicksand that it almost seems like something that only happens in the movies. I found out on Stewart Island that that's not true. When I found myself sinking into the creek at East Ruggedy Beach, I was absolutely terrified. I was lucky because only one of my legs sunk in and I managed to pull myself out.

The quicksand we have in New Zealand — wet quicksand — is actually the sand version of the liquefaction that we all heard about after the Christchurch earthquake. It's basically sand (and salt) that's got so much water in it that it can no longer support any weight. It looks like hard sand but when you step on it, you just start to sink.

The good news is that scientists don't think it's possible for your whole body to sink into quicksand, as it's *usually* less than a metre deep. The bad news is that it's often on the beach and you could drown if you get stuck in it and the tide comes in.

To get out of quicksand, the real trick is to stay as calm as you can, and to lean right back so that your weight is distributed over a bigger area, which will help you stop sinking while you work your way to the edge.

✕

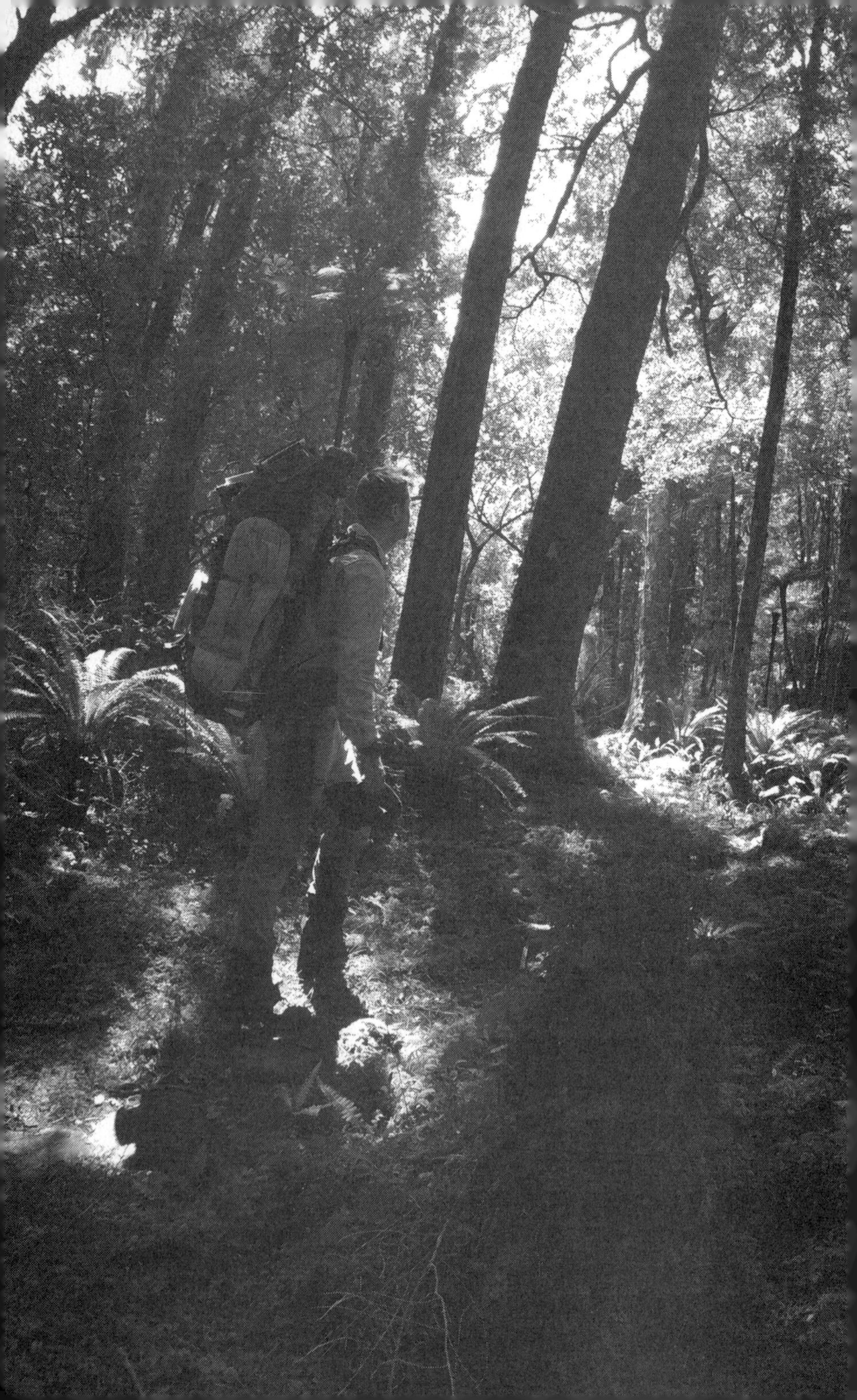

Chapter Four
DOUBT

> Day 6
> 15.11.16
> East Ruggedy Hut to Big Hellfire Hut
> 14 km

I got up at 7.45 a.m. but I didn't leave until about 9.50 — nearly an hour later than I was planning to get going, but that's pretty typical of me when I have to pack up all my stuff in the morning. I was feeling good as I'd slept really well and I had eaten plenty, too. I had more food with me for the day ahead, including the damper that I'd made and some leftover mashed potato and paua.

SURPRISINGLY, IT TOOK ME until day six to pick myself up a stick to walk with. I have a habit of becoming very attached to my walking sticks.

The plan for the day was to head to Big Hellfire Hut, which was about nine hours away. The start of the day was really windy, but thankfully the previous night's heavy rain had stopped so I wasn't going to get wet.

The first part of the track went around the back of the headland between East and West Ruggedy beaches. It then shot up into the bush. I climbed all the way to 240 metres above sea level. It was very muddy up there — my boots were completely caked in mud.

The headland reaches out into the Ruggedy Passage, which runs between Stewart Island and the Rugged Islands. Whoever named this place must have run out of ideas by the time they got here!

The track down onto West Ruggedy Beach was amazing. It was steep and on hard-packed sand. I felt almost like I was in the desert. The beach itself had soft, golden sand and barrelling waves, which — if they'd been a bit warmer — would have been brilliant for a surf. This was an epic part of my walk. It was incredibly beautiful, totally wild and there was no one else there.

On the beach, I went up to the northern end to check out a cave that I'd read about while I was in the hut the night before. Up off the beach, through the long grass, in a massive rock face, I found an opening. I'd heard right — there definitely was a cave but it was set up almost like a little hut. There were a couple of fishing buoys hanging just outside the entrance, and inside was a fireplace (complete with metal chimney), a couple of bed frames slung with fishing nets, a shelf made out of an old crate and a little table with some seats. It was all made out of stuff that had washed up on the beach. It was so cool. I almost wished I'd known about it the night before so I could have stayed there — but then I wouldn't have found all that food.

The beach was about 2.5 kilometres long and it took me a while to cover it. I don't usually enjoy walking on sand much but this was just so beautiful, I was absolutely fizzing.

The one downside was the amount of rubbish there was along the beach. That surprised me — and really pissed me off. There I was on this gorgeous beach in the middle of nowhere and there shouldn't have been any sign of other people at all. But there was heaps of it. It was all fishing waste — ropes, floats, buoys, buckets, fishing trays — disgusting. I wanted to go back and clean the place up. I'd love to go back with the Wildgirl sometime and get DOC's help to helicopter all the crap off the beach.

Once I got off the beach, the track turned inland for a bit to avoid having to climb Red Head Peak. That's not to say that the way I went was flat — I still had to cross the Ruggedy Mountains before I could stop for the night.

I noticed that there was a lot more moss on the trees and on the ground. I had obviously made it into a much wetter part of Stewart Island. More rain meant more mud — and this stuff was way worse than what I'd seen a couple of days ago. In some places, I was almost up to my knees in the stuff. My stick got put to very good use as I dragged myself through huge patches of mud.

In the back of my mind all the time was 'what if?' Some of the downhills were steep and ridiculously slippery — so steep that I felt like my knees could hyperextend and fold in half with each step.

As I climbed up the mountains, I decided that once I got to the top of one steep climb, I'd stop and take a break for lunch. As I stopped for that well-earned rest, I noticed a flash of bright colour further down the track. It attracted my attention because, for several days, all I had seen were the greens and browns of the bush. I couldn't believe my eyes.

The bright colour was the electric blue plastic of a chair, which was drilled onto a tree! I raced down to take a closer look. It was almost like someone had put it there just for me to have a rest. Almost as soon as I thought that, I wondered how many other people had had that exact same thought as they'd come over the hill. It really made me laugh.

I sat down there and ate my paua, mashed potato and damper. I'll never know who put it there or how they got it there, but I'm really glad that they did. It was just what I needed.

As I climbed higher, the track came out of the bush and into more sub-alpine scrub. There were massive granite rocks all over the place, so I did a bit of rock climbing to check out the views. If it had been a clear day, they would have been epic, but there was low, foggy cloud hanging around. I could still just make out where I'd come from and could see a bit further down the coast towards Waituna Bay.

I dropped down onto the beach there — literally, as I slipped in the sand and landed on my arse. Thankfully, I didn't damage any of my gear or myself. While I was down there, I decided it was time to try my luck diving for paua. One thing was for certain — I wasn't going to stay in the water any longer than I needed to. This was a wild piece of coast and I was only too aware of the cold and of those damn sharks!

And you know what the worst part of getting naked and going into freezing-cold, possibly shark-infested water was? I didn't get a single paua. Nothing! This was my last attempt to get paua for a while as the sea on the west coast is so brutal that I couldn't get in the water safely.

Luckily, I'd caught a rat. I'd set a trap the night before at East Ruggedy. I had put it just outside the window of the hut, and it went off at about 4 a.m. I found quite a big rat in it. I hoped it was the one that had been eating the butter because I thought that would make it a bit tastier. I'd gutted and skinned it after I caught it, and had had it in my bag all day, marinating in salt and pepper. (I later tried marinating another rat with the flavour sachet from a packet of instant noodles. Yum!)

Not having got any paua made me think about food again. But instead of feeling sad about what I didn't have I started having some crazy-cool ideas of things I could invent. Freeze-dried cream. Would that work? Freeze-dried sushi. Yes, please! Let's make that happen . . .

By four in the afternoon, I was screwed. I had another hour to go to get to the hut, but the combination of the hills and the mud had taken its toll on me. Even so, I was having a lot of fun and dinner and a bed were not far away.

Big Hellfire Hut sits up on a ridge above Big Hellfire Beach. I've heard it's called Hellfire because when the sun's setting you get this beautiful blood-red sky that looks like the fires of hell — or something like that. To get to it, I had to cross a big, open sand bowl. When I stepped out of the bush into the wind it was really blowing so I got hammered by flying sand, then before I knew it I was back in the lush green native bush.

When I got to the hut, I lit the fire and started to think about food. It had only taken me seven days, and here I was finally having to eat rat. I had no other protein and I wanted to save as many of my freeze-dried meals as I could.

I heated up some oil and browned my marinated rat in it. Then I made a little nest for it in the fire, and put the whole pan in there so that the meat roasted. While it was roasting, I put some water in my other pan and put it on the fire to heat up so I could use some of the potato flakes.

When I pulled the sizzling pan out of the fire, it sounded delicious — it didn't smell too good but the sizzling sounded fantastic! I was surprised that the roast rat also looked really good — but then, I was really hungry. The outside of it was crispy and it looked a bit like roast duck. That's what I told myself anyway. I served the rat in a sea of sloppy mashed potato — I called the dish Swimming Rat.

I started off small with one of the hind legs and — holy! — it was really good. In fact, I'm not sure why you can't buy them in supermarkets. In a matter of minutes, there was just a little pile of bones on my plate. It tasted soft and buttery. Rats eat both plants and animals but out there it's probably mostly seeds and plants, so it didn't taste too gamey, and I knew it hadn't been eating garbage. The meat was really lean.

The hut had a spectacular view to the valley below. Down there was a massive big flat area called Ruggedy Flat. It was made up of a whole lot of swamps, which in turn were the headwaters of the Freshwater River. It

When I pulled the sizzling pan out of the fire, it sounded delicious — it didn't smell too good but the sizzling sounded fantastic! I was surprised that the roast rat also looked really good — but then, I was really hungry.

was absolutely amazing to look down on, and I would have liked to have explored it but I had other plans that involved going completely off-track and into the wild.

That night I realised it was five days until my birthday. Normally, my birthday would be spent with my loved ones, my family and my friends. But this year I was going to be on my own. It was going to be interesting. I was kind of looking forward to it and kind of not. I wished there was someone sending me a birthday cake but I knew that wasn't going to happen!

I was alone at the hut. This had also been my first day without contact with the outside world because there was no phone coverage, and I was pretty lonely. I decided this would definitely be my last solo expedition ever. I'd learnt that the one real secret to my life is love, and I need that human contact. Although I love the bush, I need human love.

After dinner, I sat and read a book — believe it or not! It was called *On the Road* by Jack Kerouac. After that I wrote in my diary and thought a bit about how the trip was going. I was feeling all right, which I put down to the amount of food I'd eaten, plus the fact that I was starting to get back into the swing of things. The following day I was heading for Mason Bay and I hoped that there'd be some food there for me.

DOC huts

The Department of Conservation has heaps of huts all over the country. Some of them — like on the Great Walks — are super popular so it's a good idea to book them in plenty of time if you're planning to use them. There's heaps of others that you don't need to book, though, but you still need to buy hut tickets to 'pay' for them when you visit. It doesn't cost much per night, and this money goes towards keeping the huts in good condition. Check them out on the DOC website (www.doc.govt.nz).

There's about 950 huts from Lane Cove Hut in Northland right down to South Pegasus Hunters' Hut on Stewart Island, so you should be able to find one that suits your next adventure quite easily.

You'll need to take your own cooking stuff and food, your own sleeping bag, and definitely take your own toilet paper.

Here's what to expect in huts, according to the DOC website:

- 'Bunks' are often multi-person sleeping platforms that allow a width of 75 centimetres per person.
- Gas cookers and fuel are not generally provided.
- Water is usually supplied from a rainwater- or

stream-filled tank. The waterborne parasite Giardia may be present. Boil all water for 3 minutes before use if you are unsure of the quality.
- ✕ An intentions (hut user) book is provided in huts. Always fill it in, as it may assist in search and rescue operations. It also lets DOC know how often a hut is used.
- ✕ Huts popular with hunters may have meat safes and/or dog kennels, which are located away from the hut.
- ✕ Candle holders are provided at most huts where lighting is not provided.

✕

Day 7
16.11.16
Big Hellfire Hut to Mason Bay Hut
15 km

THE WEATHER WAS SHOCKING when I woke up. It was so windy and there was so much rain I didn't want to get out of bed. But I had to. I was heading to Mason Bay Hut today, which I figured would take about seven hours. Walking in the bad weather would make it more challenging.

I set off from Big Hellfire Hut earlier than normal, at 8.30 a.m. I decided I would spend a day or two at Mason Bay Hut to let my body recover and hopefully eat plenty of the food which had been brought in for me.

It had rained so much overnight that I decided it was time to break out my new rain jacket for the first time. The best thing about it was this little cord around the neck that you could tighten even if you weren't wearing the hood. The worst thing when you're wearing a jacket in the rain is when you have the hood down and you get water all down your neck! And boy, did it rain. The mud was even worse today. There were fresh puddles sitting on top of it. Everything was wet and muddy.

To add to the rain and the mud, I had decided to walk without eating so I could save my food for the next day. It didn't take long before my mood dropped. The main thing that was on my mind was the south coast. I'm not going to lie — I was nervous about it. It was going to be hard.

The weight of my pack was worrying me, too. I'd been struggling with the pressure it was putting on my back so I tried to think of things I could leave behind at the next hut before I ventured off into the wild.

The one bright spot among the rain and mud were the birds. I've never heard birdlife like it — even in the rain, the tui sang their hearts out.

The route from Big Hellfire to Mason Bay was on the flat tops overlooking the ocean — not that I could see much of it, as the low cloud met the fog, meaning I could only vaguely make out the landmarks ahead of me.

From Big Hellfire, I climbed about 300 metres to reach the highest point for the day, then traversed the top of a range of hills that were covered in low, sub-alpine scrub before dropping back down to sea level at Little Hellfire

Beach. Despite the name, Little Hellfire is actually bigger than Big Hellfire Beach.

When the track started heading down, it began getting dangerously steep. It was so muddy and there was still so much rain. I was slipping with almost every step. The possibility of injuring myself was very real.

Fortunately, walking along the beach gave my body a bit of a break. The rain stopped briefly, but the wind was still furious. I was enjoying the walk until I realised something terrible — I'd lost my hiking stick. I thought back and realised that I hadn't been carrying it all morning. I must have left it back at the hut. That put a real downer on what was otherwise a beautiful part of my day.

At the southern end of the beach, I stopped and filled my water pouch in a little waterfall before attacking the solid climb up and around the back of Mason Head. I thought that climb would be easy. I was so wrong. It went up and up. I eventually got to the top of the hill, but by this stage I was so tired I had to sit down every 10 minutes.

The wind made walking slow going along the exposed parts of the track so I was happy to get back into the bush. Well, I say happy but actually my brain was somewhere else entirely.

I couldn't get my mind off the south coast. I thought about it constantly. I was terrified. I felt like I might have set myself up for failure. I argued with myself. How could I say that when I hadn't even seen it yet? I hadn't been there. I didn't know what it was like. But my mind really wanted me to say 'Time to go home!' My body was exhausted, so it agreed with the part of my mind that was telling me to stop.

But there was another part of me that knew I needed to carry on, that I needed to at least find out what it was going to be like before I made any kind of decision. I had to try to carry on to the best of my ability and as safely as I could. Even as I was thinking all of these things, I knew that the fact I hadn't eaten all day was a big reason why I was feeling so confused.

RIGHT ON MIDDAY, something great happened. As I was walking, there was a gap in the trees where sun was streaming through. It shook me out of my dark mood and I took some time to just stand in that sunny spot and lap up the light.

My first sight of the famous Mason Bay was amazing. The bay is about 12 kilometres long and it sweeps around in a big semicircle. I was headed to the hut, which meant walking about 4 kilometres up the beach, before turning inland and heading up Duck Creek for about 1 kilometre.

That all sounds straightforward, but first I had to get down to the beach. The track was super steep and very slippery — and muddy, of course. By this stage, one of my boots was giving me a bit of a hard time so I had to stop a few times to adjust the laces.

Down on the beach, the waves were pumping and the wind was still blowing hard — so hard that I had to rescue my hat from a tree at one point. Losing my stick and my hat in one day would really have sucked. Things didn't improve much from there. The beach was a mixture of sandy bits that I could cover quite quickly, and really rocky bits that slowed me down a lot. Crossing one rocky bit, I managed to trip and drop my water pouch, losing all my water for the day. I was gutted!

The tide was at its highest, so I couldn't get around the bottom of the cliff. I followed the high-tide track straight up a vertical sand dune. It was horrible. Anyone who's ever tried doing that will know that for every step you take forward you slide back a little. That felt like pretty much what I'd been doing all day. Combine that with being sand-blasted by the wind and I wasn't happy out there. My knees were very sore and my shoulders were killing me.

When I made it to the turn-off up the creek to the hut, I was limping quite badly and couldn't wait to get to shelter — but I had a couple of stream crossings to do and a few more sand dunes to climb first. By the time I hit the grassy track leading to the hut, I was shattered. It had been a big day for me both physically and mentally.

Then, almost like magic, I could hear voices shouting and laughing through the bush. I'd forgotten that the kids from Halfmoon Bay School were going to be at the hut on their school camp. Fantastic! That lifted my spirits straight away.

They were all excited to see me, so once I'd dropped my pack, I headed outside to play some games with them. It was great to be doing something just for the fun of it. I hadn't had much fun over the past few days, that's for sure. We played and then I had dinner with them —

sausages and damper. I even made a sausage wrapped in damper, which I cooked over the fire. That was awesome. It was cool to spend some more time with these kids. After dinner, they all found sticks and toasted marshmallows over a small fire. It was awesome — and those gooey, sticky, hot, sugary marshmallows were delicious.

It had been a hard but good day. I realised that I was almost a quarter of the way around the island. It had been hard work but I was feeling really good after hanging out with a cool bunch of people. Even better than that, Dad had been in touch with the teachers and arranged for them to bring a whole bunch more food in for me. That was going to make things a bit easier.

There was only one more hut before I went into the wilderness, so I was looking forward to having a couple of days at Mason Bay to rest and for my body to recover. I had welts on my shoulders and hips from my pack. I was still nervous about the next stage but as long as I had food and shelter I'd be sweet.

Day 8
17.11.16
Mason Bay Hut (rest day)

I WOKE UP AT around 7.30 a.m. to one of the kids yelling '*Breakfast!*' Not for me, though. Today was about resting. I felt like I should be walking but I didn't want to move, so I rolled over and went back to sleep.

At 8.30 I got up and went into the kitchen and started

making some rolled oats to eat. (Some kind hunters had left them behind.) I added a dash of golden syrup, too. Man, it was good. I knew my food levels would drop again the next day when I set off to Doughboy Bay Hut.

Having a rest day was great. I got out my maps and thought some more about the whole south coast thing. I worked out a couple of break points and also a possible alternative route. I'd done a lot of thinking and talked to a few locals and, as a result, had changed my plan. I had been going to stick right to the coast but I realised that that just wasn't going to be physically possible. It's just too cliffy and too bluffy.

There was a DOC worker, Mike, who was on the school camp with the kids. I spent quite a bit of time talking to him about what I was planning to do. He took one look at the short gaiters I had on over my boots and said, 'They won't do!' He gave me a pair of his that not only covered my boots but went right up to my knees. He reckoned I would need them more than he did.

Mike had spent some time working down towards the south coast, cat-trapping and monitoring the endangered southern New Zealand dotterel. He told me that I should go up over the tops instead, as he'd done some trapping up there and it was easier than the coast. As a result, I marked a route on my map that went slightly further inland than I had planned in parts. That made me feel a bit better — still nervous, but a bit better.

The rain had stopped and even though it was still quite windy, it was actually a nice day. I headed down to the beach to meet the team from the TV show *Seven*

Sharp, who had flown in on a small plane and landed on the beach. I talked a bit about how this was an emotional journey and an emotional step on the way to me becoming a man. I laughed and said, 'I don't do things the easy way! This is just so isolated, I'm really going to get the opportunity to learn about myself.'

I was trying my best to sound super confident about what I was planning but I think my nervousness showed through when I described the bit of my route after the track as being 'gnarly scrub, and nothing but scrub, hills and bush. Urrrghhh'.

It was weird to think of people watching me on television when I was so far out of the loop with what was happening in the world and even basic communication was really difficult. Once they left, I realised that I was now on my own for sure. There would be no more food drops, no more company and no more relying on anyone else until I was out the other side. It all started to seem a bit real.

The TV crew had managed to bring my new BioLite stove from Dad. I was stoked. I now had more freeze-dried meals and a whole bunch of other stuff — rice, flour, things like that. It was a relief to restock my supplies.

There was a hunters' hut a couple of kilometres away from the main Mason Bay Hut, so I decided to stash some of the food there. It was the only place I could think of that I'd be able to get back to if I needed to — plus I didn't really want to carry it all with me, as I had too much stuff already. I didn't plan to come back to it but I knew it was there if I needed it.

Throughout the rest of the day I tested out my new BioLite. It's a stove that generates electricity off burning wood. How amazing is that? It's insane. I was feeling way more confident about my battery capacity with this new item on board.

I also made a whole lot of bread. When the kids left to go back to Oban, they left me with some flour so I made three loaves of damper. It was some damn fine bread, the best I'd ever made.

I ate dinner, then, at about 8.30 p.m., I decided to run up this huge sand dune to watch the sun set. Even though I'd already eaten, I took a packet meal with me and ate as I watched the sunset across the sand. Some of the dunes have these crazy-looking layers and some are all round and smooth. Being up there was like being on another planet.

I carried on climbing the dunes after the sun set, as it was still really light. The view from the top was incredible — it took in the whole of the bay towards the wild in the south and Mason Head to the north. As I skidded my way happily back down the dunes, I felt like a kid playing in the sand. It was so great!

I did a video diary outside on the edge of the dunes at 9.15 p.m.

Alrighty! I spent the day resting and recovering. I've been feeling a little lethargic today. I felt like I needed to be walking. But I didn't want to move. Haha! I'm worried about the loneliness that's looming over my head. Tomorrow I'm heading to Doughboy Bay Hut, my last bit

I knew that up ahead was pure wilderness and, like it or not, that was where I was headed.

of civilisation (well, kind of, it's just a hut in the middle of nowhere). I miss my family . . . but there's nothing I can do about that. I guess I know they love me so that will have to do. Ahhh . . . the wild is close. Goodnight.

> Day 9
> 18.11.16
> Mason Bay Hut to Doughboy Bay Hut
> 18 km

I WOKE UP FEELING not too good. I was about to go into No Man's Land. There was no way I could really pull out — not that I wanted to — but it would have been so nice to be at home snuggled on the couch with my girlfriend and the dog. This time it was proper worry, since I had had breakfast and had a full tummy. This was 'The Day Before Shit Gets Real'.

The plan for the day was to head over to Doughboy Bay Hut, which would take about seven hours or so. I headed back down to the beach, this time to walk another 5 or 6 kilometres of it before heading up to the tops again then dropping down to the hut at Doughboy Bay. At Mason Bay, I left the North West Circuit as it headed back inland, and carried on along the Southern Circuit track.

My nervousness wasn't helped by a chance meeting I had with a couple of hunters at the hut where I planned to leave my food. They definitely didn't make me feel any better by talking about just how tough the terrain was where I was going. They told me I was crazy. I walked away from them thinking that maybe they were right.

But I felt I didn't have a choice because I said I'd do it.

I put on a brave face for those men, but not long after we parted, I was struggling. My pack was so heavy my shoulders and hips were killing me. I broke down in tears screaming, 'I don't know what I'm doing!' I heard it echo in the distance. I was so nervous and upset about what I was about to do. Up ahead was pure wilderness and, like it or not, that was where I was headed.

I quickly realised that I needed a new mental approach so I didn't get trapped by my apprehension. I decided to break the trip down into smaller goals to make it easier to accomplish.

The first of the goals was to make it down to Magog and Gog, two prominent features made of granite that stick up in the southwest of the island. My goal was to make it to them and, from there, I'd set a new goal.

My newfound optimism didn't last very long. I tried to focus on the new plan but my mind kept going back to just how big and stupid this whole project was. I soon found myself having a complete meltdown. I couldn't hold back the tears as I shouted 'What am I doing?' into the wind. I trudged along, crying and swearing. I guess I was trying to make sense of why I was on this isolated beach at the bottom of the world.

A couple of hours later, and back in the bush, I'd worked out a few things. I'd recalled that the last time I'd gone off on a big adventure it had been easy, because I had had nothing much to leave behind. My life had been a mess and whatever happened on my walk had to be better than what I would have been doing at home, which was smoking, drinking and being a bit of an arsehole. This time, though, I had a life — a home, a girlfriend, friends — and I'd walked away from all of that to do something crazy and adventurous and fun. The only problem was that I was in this horrid headspace where I thought I wasn't having any fun at all.

I spent ages trying to decide whether I could or should change the objectives of my adventure so that I could at least get some enjoyment out of it, rather than trying to be the first person to walk around the island. I needed to do what was right by me. Was I just doing this because I'd said I would, rather than because I really wanted to?

I'm always telling people to do what they love, to do what makes them happy, so why was I doing something that was making me so unhappy? Why was I doing something I knew I wasn't going to enjoy? I might not have had the answers but at least I'd worked out what the questions were, I guess.

The highest point of the day — Adams Hill — was about 400 metres above sea level. It was ridiculously steep and so muddy. My pack was heavier because of all the food I was carrying and I was struggling. I started crying and talking to myself. Then this guy Andrew, who I'd met at the hut the night before, walked up behind me. I was a bit embarrassed because he would have heard all the stuff I'd been saying. I had to snap out of the sad mood I was in and act 'normal'. He was a fisherman, and we talked about his job, his boat and how much he loved going hunting. Every opportunity he got, he'd take off around the island for some time away.

I talked about how I was feeling about the coast. He sensed that I was really fearful. He told me it would be hard work but I'd be fine. It helped to ease my nerves. He was heading to Doughboy Bay as well, so it was good to know I'd have some company.

On the top of Adams Hill, Andrew carried on but I stopped and looked south across Doughboy Bay and into the great unknown. I could make out the dark outline of the coast against the grey of the sea and the sky, and it didn't make me feel any better. Looking back towards Mason Head and the Ernest Islands offshore made me wish I could go back to the safety of the known and the familiar. But in the back of my mind I could feel a small part of me was excited, and being drawn into the wild.

The tops were open, exposed and bloody windy (and, yes, still muddy!). But they did offer one unexpected bonus — cellphone coverage. It turned out that I was high above a river valley that led back east to Paterson Inlet and further beyond to Oban. The cell signal from Oban somehow magically made it all the way out here and I was able to call Ngaio.

Just hearing her voice made me feel so much better. She told me to just keep my head up and keep on trucking on. That was exactly what I needed to hear. She was so kind to me. I felt so much better about everything after talking to her. I told her that I was coming home — but slowly!

WHEN I GOT TO Doughboy and read 'Quicksand' on the map, I thought 'Oh no!' I knew that I'd be OK on dry sand, but when you're on saturated sand it's dangerous. I had to cross a river and was expecting to suddenly disappear into a hole.

The first bit of sand was solid and there were a few other sets of footprints on it, so I knew I wasn't alone. I stopped for a bit and used a stick to write 'I love my life!' in the sand. I'm not sure that I really believed it, though.

The bay itself was awesome. The headland to the north sticks out so far that it looks like it almost joins onto the land to the south. That means that it's fairly well protected so the wind and waves weren't quite as crazy as on other parts of the coast.

When I got to the hut, Andrew and another hunter were already there. The hut had this weird little gate on the verandah that none of the other huts I'd stayed in had had — which turned out to be for stopping sea lions from getting in!

I set up my BioLite on the verandah and tried to take in the view. I was feeling stressed, sore and broken this far into the journey, and I thought that it was only going to get worse.

Chapter Five
STRUGGLE

> Day 10
> 19.11.16
> Doughboy Bay Hut to Deceit Peaks
> 5 km

My video diary for the morning read:

Today is 'shit hits the fan' day. Shit's about to get real day. Shit's going to get thick day.

I'm headed off into the bush in about an hour. I'm going to walk up a ridge and then follow it for a couple of days, then drop down into a swamp. Up onto another ridge, follow it for a couple of days then hopefully by then I'll be at the Gogs — Gog and Magog, two peaks on the southern part of the island — within four or five days. It's going to be a long four to five days. I'm going to get pissed off. I'm going to get upset but eventually I'm going to pop out where I want to, fingers crossed.

I'm feeling pretty damn nervous. I'm not feeling good. I'm starting to question why I've decided to do this but I think it will be fun (once it's over!).

I'm slowly going to run out of food over the next week. And then the week after I'm going to run out of even more food. Yeah. This is where it gets real. No more of this pussying about on a track.

WHEN I GOT UP, Andrew had already left to head down to the old settlement at the other end of the beach. I was a bit sad to have missed him, so left him a note on the table. I ate some muesli for breakfast, took one final look at my maps and finished packing my stuff. I slowly climbed into my wet boots and put on my pack. I set off out onto the beach at about 9.30 a.m.

This was it. This was where the real adventure began.

From Doughboy Bay Hut, the Southern Circuit carries on for about 500 metres along the beach before turning inland and tracking the length of the Rakeahua River back to Paterson Inlet. That 500 metres of beach was to be my last walk on marked trail for . . . I didn't know how long.

After the track turned off into the hills, I carried on down the beach towards the river crossing. The wind was so strong that it had blown a whole lot of foam off the sea right up the beach. It looked almost like snow.

The river crossing was a bit of a worry as I thought there might be more quicksand. Thankfully, I got through it OK. On the other side of the river there were lots of whale bones from a stranding in 2015. Some trampers found 29 pilot whales beached but couldn't alert DOC until they walked out. By the time the rangers got there, it was too late and all they could do was leave nature to take its course. Seeing all the bones made me think back to the days when whalers would chase their prey into the bay and kill them. It was so sad to see those bones and think about the whales being killed. I also thought about how tough life must have been for the old whalers.

I looked up to see Andrew again, a bit further along the beach. He said he'd had a little look along there to see if he could find any tracks but he couldn't see anything. He walked with me to the end of the beach. I tried to talk him into coming with me, because I didn't want to do it on my own. He was real keen at first but I think he was just kidding me. When I asked if he was sure he didn't want to come, he said, 'This is your journey, mate!'

At the end of the beach was a hole in the rock that I walked through. It reminded me so much of Cathedral Cove in the Coromandel. It felt familiar, but this was my gateway into the unknown at the same time.

The beach on the other side of it was where I took my first steps into the wild. It was also the first place where I got out my compass. I was going to need it to work out where I was and where I was heading — no more following the orange triangles and the yellow and green signs that had helpfully been provided by DOC for the last few days. From now on, I was on my own — just me and the bush.

I headed up the hill south of Doughboy Bay and straight in amongst it from there. This was the bit I had been dreading. I took off up a steep bank and was almost instantly bush-bashing.

When I first went in, I was so stoked. I was finally doing it! The scrub wasn't that bad. I had to push through a little bit but then it opened up. I thought, 'This is all good!'

Then I carried on a bit and it got a bit thicker. 'I'm all right.' Then suddenly it got so thick that I could hardly move. 'I can deal with this.' I kept going, pushing through it. I made my way up and up and up.

My thoughts about what the south-coast bush would look like back on day four turned out to be far from true

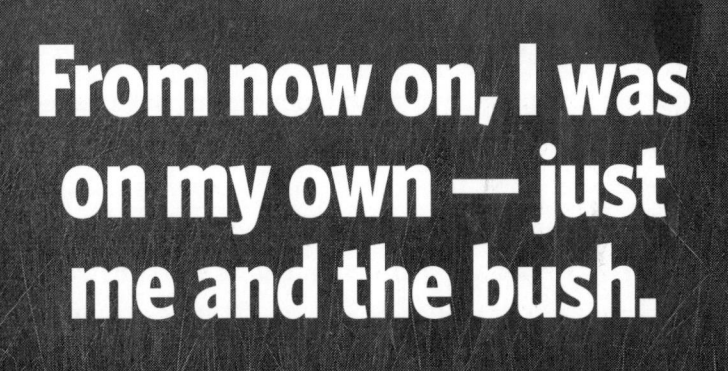

From now on, I was on my own — just me and the bush.

— the reality was much worse. The bush was thick and I had to make my way through thousands of skinny little trees all growing in big tangles. I had to really bash my way through it.

I got to this little clearing after I'd been going for a couple of hours. It was so windy and I was wet as it had started raining. It took me about three hours to cover the first kilometre away from the beach. It was so slow moving through the scrub. Sticks were catching on everything. It was a nightmare. Up and down through thick and thin, plaited and open scrub. It was such hard work.

Every now and then, I'd stop and climb a tree to see if I could get a vantage point to help me work out where I was going — but mostly all I could see was more trees.

Somewhere along the way, I came up with this little saying: 'Life lesson one from the bush: always take the path of least resistance — but, as much as you can, travel on the track less travelled.' I interpret that as meaning you should always try to take the easy-going path, while making sure there is lots to explore.

Eventually I made it onto the tops. At around 300 metres elevation there were suddenly lots of open paths made by the wind. The scrub was thinner — there were just low sub-alpine plants, so I could move a bit faster, interspersed with patches of flax and bushes that were around the same height as I was. This was super annoying as I spent a lot of time getting smacked in the face by bits of tree and flax. It was also super windy — blowing 20 to 25 knots an hour.

I had decided my goal for the day was to get to the

base of the Deceit Peaks. This was a good motivator, as whenever I was on open ground I could see the peaks rising in the distance.

The weird thing about today was that my brain was in quite a good place. I'd spent so long worrying about what it was going to be like once I left the track that I'd turned it into a really huge barrier in my head. Once I actually did go into the wild, I found I could stop worrying about it. I could spend all my time and energy focused on where I was and what I was doing right now, rather than thinking too much about what was ahead.

As I dropped down into the bush again, I found things changed a lot. I got stuck in the middle of a whole lot of thick scrub. I used my knife to try to cut through some of it but it took so long it hardly seemed worth it. I bashed and crashed my way through, constantly getting hit in the face by sticks and getting cuts all over my head, hands and legs. I actually couldn't move in that stuff. It was awful. It took me ages to move forward just a few metres. At some points, it seemed like it would be quicker to get down on my hands and knees and crawl under the scrub, but that wasn't always possible.

I made it to the awesome granite landscape of Deceit Peaks. There were huge mountains made of granite towering over me, and big boulders that made me wish I had my climbing shoes. It was unlike anything I had ever seen. The granite covered the landscape and boulders the size of houses were somehow balancing on the top of the peaks. The only logical explanation is that giants put them there!

I thought, right, this is where I'm going to camp. I found a little pocket in some scrub down in a little hollow and set up my tent. I was looking forward to spending my first night in the middle of one of the wildest places I had ever been.

I got the BioLite going to make dinner. My water was just about hot when the sky went very dark. Five minutes later it started hailing. Then came the thunder and lightning. Thankfully, it didn't last too long, and I soon had hot water to rehydrate a meal for my dinner. I ate that and climbed into my tent hoping for a good night's sleep. It was good to have that little bit of protection from the wind.

I'd been walking all day and had only managed to cover about 5 kilometres. It was probably the hardest day of my life in terms of getting from A to B. Absolutely everything under the sun was between me and where I wanted to go. Trees, dirt, scrub, mud, rivers — you name it, it was there. Hard work, let me tell you. The gnarliness of the terrain had really challenged me.

It started raining as I settled into the tent but I was feeling good now that I'd started this stage of the expedition. Each morning, I'd switch on the satellite phone and quickly check the weather forecast. There was supposed to be some bad weather coming, which I wasn't too excited about. In fact, I thought it would be nice if it didn't come at all.

I decided that the next morning, I would climb the ridge just above me to check out where I was going. I was feeling way better than I had a few days ago.

Before I went to sleep, I used my satellite phone to let Ngaio know I was OK, and to get an updated forecast. It had been a great day mentally, even though my body was wrecked.

Day 11
20.11.16
Deceit Peaks to the middle of nowhere
6 km

HAPPY BIRTHDAY TO ME! I woke up in one of the coolest places I had ever been, but I was on my own. I missed my family and my girlfriend.

I put a candle on a piece of damper and sang myself Happy Birthday, then ate my birthday bread for breakfast with a little bit of butter. I followed that up with some hot milk made from milk powder, an apple and an orange.

That was a pretty special birthday breakfast for me. If it hadn't been so goddamn cold, it would have been the best place I'd ever had a birthday — but it was freaking freezing.

I hadn't slept well because of the cold. If I could help it, this would be the last time I camped at this elevation in my little summer-weight sleeping bag. I had slept in all of my clothes and was still cold. I reckon it was about zero degrees before adding in the wind-chill factor.

It took me a while to pack up and get moving. My goal for the day was just to head further south. First I headed up to the ridge I'd sussed the previous night to get a good view of where I needed to go. I could see some flats at the bottom of a valley, so that's where I was headed.

The rain fell in waves. It would come and go, always from the west. The wind hadn't stopped. It felt like it never did. It blew and blew. All the trees were hardened and hunched over by the weather, which made them terrible to walk through.

Once I started walking, it started to hail quite heavily again. I don't know if you've ever walked along in gnarly-as winds with massive hailstones getting smashed sideways into your face, but it's not fun. At least I was high enough up that I didn't have to bash my way through too much bush for a while.

After a couple of hours, I had to drop back down into the scrub. It was as horrible as it had been the day before, and it stretched for miles and miles. I would not wish it on my worst enemy. I was so desperate to get out of the scrub that when I came to a small river, I decided to climb into it and follow it for as long as I could. It was freezing cold but at least I didn't have to bush-bash while I was in there. Eventually, I had to climb back out and into the scrub, so then I was hacking my way through almost impenetrable forest *and* I was really wet. I couldn't even navigate using the waterways because there were thousands of them. If I followed one it would just disappear into a tarn. This was so not fun.

There were patches that were incredibly clear of vegetation and all I was doing was finding the path with the least scrub between those spots. I could often see the next clear patch from the previous one and I'd head towards it. They were all really wet so I couldn't camp on them. I think they had nothing growing in them because they were the spots where the water table was a bit higher.

When I made it to the odd patch of open land covered in sub-alpine grass and a few small shrubs, I really took the time to appreciate it — especially when I could spot a deer track and follow it. I knew that if animals were taking that route then it was probably a good idea to follow it.

Speaking of deer, I got a fright that day. A deer had been sleeping behind some bushes and I walked right past it. It woke up and took off, its big white tail firing away as it ran past. That set my heart racing as I hadn't expected it at all.

I thought about how I was probably the only person anywhere down here for a very long way. Amazing. I loved being out in the open up on the tops — it felt like that was the kind of adventure that I was there for, not spending hours on end smashing my body and going nowhere.

When I finally got down to the flats, they were epic. It made me think about the fact that all of New Zealand would have been this wild once. I was dodging the tarns and crossed about three rivers. At the end of the flats I had about 2 kilometres of scrub sliding — on my hands and knees underneath the scrub — to do before I stopped for the night.

Late in the afternoon, the sun came out just as I had to cross a river. It was so nice to feel a little bit of warmth after all that rain and hail. Thankfully, there was a series of big rocks across the river and I managed to hop across

The rain fell in waves. It would come and go, always from the west. The wind hadn't stopped. It felt like it never did. It blew and blew.

them without getting too wet. They almost looked like they'd been put there so people could cross the river, but I was so far out in the middle of nowhere that that wasn't possible. It was just nature providing for me once again!

After about six hours of walking, covering about a kilometre an hour, I stopped and set up camp for the night. I pitched my tent right next to a patch of bush out on an open bit of land. The wind was still blowing hard but my little tent was up to the challenge.

I found my towel because I was going to wash myself — I stank so bad. I followed a deer track from my tent back down to the river, about 300 metres away. I stripped down all ready to jump in.

I totally failed when I tried to throw my clothes from a rock in the middle of the river to the side. I threw my underwear and the wind caught them and they fell right in the river. I quickly jumped in to get them and lost all fear of the cold water . . . but as soon as I grabbed them I realised how freezing it actually was. My skin went all tight and I got instant goosebumps — it was a serious shock for my body. I managed to stay in there for about 40 seconds, while I had a quick wash. It was my first wash in six days and I felt so clean and fresh. It was my best birthday wash ever!

Freezing, I walked back up to my tent with no pants on. It was very cold. I put on my night-time clothes and got into my tent. I was so stoked every night when I wasn't walking anymore. That was the best part of my day — having something to eat and doing stuff around the camp was great. The rest of the day it was like, 'A little bit further, a little bit further, maybe I'll stop here, maybe I'll stop there, a little bit further.'

For dinner, I fried up some of my birthday bread in coconut oil. It looked, smelled and tasted delicious. I had it with a freeze-dried meal.

All up, it had been a pretty damn good day. I felt stoked with how beautiful the landscape had been. Everything was so amazing even though it was raining and cold.

I tried to call out on the satellite phone that night but it didn't work. The reception was too patchy — I only got about three words out before I got cut off. It felt a bit weird that my first day of not talking to anyone was also my birthday.

Day 12
21.11.16
The middle of nowhere to Easy Harbour
6 km

I WOKE UP FEELING GOOD. I'd had a decent night's sleep except that my head was in a hollow, so I'd wake up every now and then with a sore neck. Lying in my tent, I heard a familiar sound — rain. Thankfully, I was in a sweet spot sheltered from the wind.

I'd saved a coffee bag that I'd grabbed from a hut and I used the last of the milk powder to make my first and last coffee with my breakfast, which was fried bread. It's the little things that make a difference when you're out in the middle of nowhere.

While I was having my coffee, I got out my map and

checked out my route for the day. I hoped to get roughly 6 kilometres down to Easy Harbour by the end of the day. I liked the thought of anything easy after the days of bush-bashing I'd done. I wasn't looking forward to another day of pushing through scrub.

In my diary, I wrote:

I'm looking forward to getting into the bush and all up in that scrub. We're pretty good friends, me and the scrub. When we were first getting to know each other, scrub and me had a bit of a falling out. My legs are completely covered with bruises. Any part of me that's below the knee has been destroyed by scrub. The branches hit my shins, it's terrible stuff.

EASY HARBOUR WAS ABOUT 6 kilometres away, and it was about 3 kilometres off the most direct route I'd worked out to get me down to the Gogs. Given that in the last two days I'd only managed 5 or 6 kilometres a day, I decided that if I got to the point where I'd have to turn off to get to the harbour and decided 'Screw this, I'm not going down there' then I'd just camp up on the ridge for the night.

Mentally, Easy Harbour had some significance for me. About a kilometre south of there was one of the 'bug-out' points that I'd set myself. It was where I'd decide whether I would carry on around the south coast or take a different course. It wasn't going to be an easy decision for me to make as I'd told so many people that I was planning to walk around the entire island.

Could I change my mind? Should I?

I set out straight into the bush. It was bush-bashing from the get-go. I quickly got back into my groove. The only difference from the day before was that the rain was heavier and more constant, but there was a little less wind.

At one point, I was making my way downhill and found myself face to face with a massive, moss-covered rock wall. That hadn't been on my map. Bloody hell! My choices were to either go back the way I had come and try to find a way around it, or to climb straight up it.

Using vines and small trees to grab onto, I slowly made my way up the slippery face, all too aware that if I fell, I was on my own. When I made it to the top, I stopped and hugged the nearest big tree I could find in grateful thanks for having made it up in one piece.

The day was all about navigation, and for the most part I did a damn good job. I didn't get lost at all. However, I got my speed/distance a bit wrong a few times: I'd drop down hills too early, thinking I'd got further than I had, then I'd just have to turn around and climb back up again.

By midday I was completely soaked. I hadn't stopped for a snack so I was starting to get cold. I stopped, ate some nuts and continued.

There was the odd bit of forest where the trees were big enough for me to walk through. When I got to them, a little part of me would hope that they marked the end of the scrub. Unfortunately, the opposite was true as mid-afternoon, I encountered a new level of scrub thickness. I found myself in the middle of what I labelled 'move-nowhere scrub'. It was like being caught in a tightly woven net of skinny, scratchy branches. It was way taller than me so I couldn't go over it, and it was growing so tightly that there was no way under it. I could see absolutely no way through it, but there was no way back either. I just had to throw myself into it and try my hardest to push my way through. This wasn't so much scrub-thumping as full-contact wrestling with it. It was so tough!

Mentally, I was on the edge. From that point it got worse and worse. I had to tell myself that everything was going to be OK. At one point I cried after singing a song that reminded me of Ngaio and her family. The loneliness was such a struggle.

As I made my way down towards Easy Harbour, there were several rivers I needed to cross. All the rain meant that they were running quite high and I had to be really careful.

My compass got a good workout that day as there were very few vantage points where I could get my bearings and see where I was heading towards. All I saw for most of the day was scrub right in my face. It was absolutely exhausting, but I felt so good when I finally got out of it. The only thing was I knew that I had potentially weeks of doing nothing but this every day if I was going to make it around the south coast.

Eventually, I reached spot height 258 (the highest point in the area according to my map) and I could see a tiny peep of the coast through the scrub — Easy Harbour! It had been anything but easy to get to but once I'd seen it, I knew I had to get there for the night.

I sidled down for about 3 kilometres to the edge of Easy Harbour. I finally made my way back down to sea level at 6 p.m. and I was so happy to be standing on a beach again. The sandy beach was quite small but just being able to walk across flat sand in the open was amazing.

My home for the night was a cave shelter just off the beach that I'd heard about from some hunters. It was open at both ends so didn't offer much shelter from the wind but at least it wasn't raining in there. Someone had hung some black plastic as a sort of door and there was a big piece of corrugated iron that was perfect for making a fire against. They had also put a stick up to hang your clothes on. I sat on a log because the old chair there looked really unstable. On the single quite flat patch there was a nice thick layer of sand so that's where I set up my tent and lit my fire.

It was such a treat to get out of the wet bush and into the shelter. I was able to dry some of my gear, which after five days of rain was quite wet. There was even a bed in the cave, made out of an old fishing net suspended from the roof, but I decided it didn't look too comfortable so I set up my tent. It was a great opportunity to dry that out, too.

The cave was total luxury. I could have stayed there for weeks. I cooked three rats that I'd caught the night before for dinner and watched the colours drain from the sky. I felt like a pirate marooned on a wild island — the only thing that was missing was a bottle of rum!

I had lit a fire in the sand but I didn't realise there was a layer of black plastic underneath it. It started to melt and somehow set some wood on fire. I had to rush back and forth getting sea water to put the fire out. It was dark and I almost tripped over a sea lion! It gave me the biggest fright. I ran back as fast as I could to grab my torch. When I went back I saw it was massive, but thankfully it was more scared of me than I was of it. It just growled a bit and took off.

While I was happy to be in the shelter, I was so tired I couldn't even think properly. I had my first-ever blister, which wasn't good. I had pack sores on my lower back and my shoulders. I had a boot sore on my left foot, which was getting gross. All my cuts were getting septic and I had these big ones on my hands. It always happens when you can't wash yourself or your things properly — you get these sores all over your body.

I had travelled just over 6 kilometres today. It was one of the hardest days I'd had so far. Looking at where I had to go the next day, I could see that it would be even harder. It wasn't far — only 2.5 kilometres — but it looked freaking steep. Not fun!

I tried to make a phone call but the atmospheric conditions were too bad so I couldn't get a connection. It was such a pain, because when I really needed to know what the weather was doing, the weather stopped me from finding out. When I didn't need to know what the weather would be doing, the conditions were perfect and the sat phone worked fine.

On the upside, I felt as if I was ahead of where I thought I would be. I had thought it was going to take me a week to get here but it had only taken three days.

It would take me one more day to get to where I wanted to go. The next day I hoped I'd make it to the Gogs, and that was exciting.

×

Seals and sea lions

While I was on Stewart Island I had a couple of close encounters with seals and sea lions. If you come across one, it's more than likely to be hanging out in the sun on a beach, having a nap, but don't let that fool you into thinking that they'll move slowly. They can really go!

They might look cute but always remember that they're wild animals with super-sharp teeth and crazy-strong jaws — the pressure of a fur seal's bite can be as much as 2 tonnes per centimetre. They will literally crush you.

On the plus side, a fur seal is quite likely to be scared of you and will usually head for the water if they can.

Which is more than can be said for a leopard seal. These guys aren't really scared of people and they'll go fifty-fifty on getting back in the water or trying to take a piece out of you (or your dog, or your kid).

Sea lions are usually pretty chilled out around people and will quite often ignore you if they're resting. If they're not napping, though, they might chase you if you get a bit close, so do your best to keep well away from them.

Here are some basic guidelines that will keep you

(and the seals) safe if you ever run into each other at the beach:

- ✗ stay at least 20 metres away
- ✗ don't disturb them by making loud noises or throwing things
- ✗ keep dogs and children away
- ✗ don't try to feed them
- ✗ never attempt to touch a seal.

Also, don't be a dickhead around these creatures. They're protected by law and it's an offence to disturb, harass, harm, injure or kill a seal — anyone charged with doing that (or letting their dog do it) could face two years in jail or a fine of up to $250,000.

✗

Day 13
22.11.16
Easy Harbour to just north of Magog
3.8 km

HARDEST DAY YET. I spent the best part of the morning cleaning up my gear. I had enjoyed my time in this little bay. It was nice to be in a shelter to stop the rain from wetting everything. It was about 10 a.m. when I finally left.

I was really sad to leave my little campsite in the cave, but from the beach I could see the dark peak of the Gog

I felt like a pirate marooned on a wild island — the only thing that was missing was a bottle of rum!

and I was determined to get there so I could tick off my first goal. I'd only been going a few minutes when I got my boots wet. Damn — wet boots to start the day is not fun.

As I made my way along the rocks at the end of the beach, I had a little company. For once, it wasn't a rat — I was walking with a little yellow-eyed penguin! I watched as it hopped along the rocks and then jumped into the sea and swam gracefully away. So cool!

I was much less graceful as I hauled myself up over some massive boulders so I could get a bit further around the coast. Even all the way down here, there was a whole lot of rubbish from fishing boats along the beach. Man, that made me mad.

Then it was straight into the world's worst scrub. It was not funny at all. I could hardly move!

Until I hit the wild, I thought a lot about what people at home were doing. Each night on my video diary, I would talk about what I thought Ngaio and my family were up to. I got homesick thinking about it. Once I hit the wild, I didn't have time to think about them. I had to fully focus on what I was doing each day. It was serious navigation — I had to focus on my map and compass. I'd set a bearing, walk for a couple of hours, find a high point and reset my bearing. In the scrub, I'd climb to the top of a tree or a rocky outcrop so I could get a sight line and so I had space to open my map.

Fortunately, the rain had stopped and there was a little bit of sunshine. Once I got up the hill above Easy Harbour, the view back was spectacular: islands and hills covered in lush green bush, sparkling blue water and that little sandy bay beautiful under a blue sky — and there, in the distance, was the Gog. Yes! That's where I was going, no matter how long it took me to get there.

It soon became apparent that it was going to take a very long time, as I was straight back into the scrub. Not just any scrub — the famous 'move-nowhere scrub' was back. It was wind-broken, so it was hard and sharp. As I walked through it, it poked holes in my clothes and ripped my skin. I had this constant fear of falling over and being impaled on one of the sharp, hard sticks.

Somewhere in the scrub, I lost my knife. That was a game changer. I realised that I'd lost it shortly after it happened, but I couldn't turn back and retrace my steps because I'd never find it in that scrub.

After I'd been going for about three hours, I cracked. I'd had enough. I sat down and cried. The tears flowed as I tried to work out what to do. My body was cut, bleeding and seriously bruised, and my mind had been wrecked all because of this unrelenting scrub. I just wanted to go home. I'd lost my knife. I'd lost my snorkel. I'd lost one of my lights. I was stuck in the fucking scrub. Ahhhh! I screamed, I swore and I cried my heart out.

Eventually, the tears stopped. I had to keep going. Minutes later, as I was climbing a big rock, I lost my footing and slid back down to the bottom. Thankfully, I wasn't injured but it was so infuriating. I just felt like nothing was going right.

An hour later, I popped out on a little beach. It felt like I had gone so far but as I looked back along the coast I saw I had only travelled about 600 metres. My heart sank as I looked along the coast ahead. I dropped my pack, not wanting to go back in the scrub.

It was horrible. It broke me. Why was I putting myself through this? In the battle between Stewart Island and Wildboy, it was becoming clear that Stewart Island was always going to win. How did I end up in a fight with this beautiful place? That was never part of the plan. I didn't want to fight the place — I wanted to see it, experience it, be part of it.

After a little self-motivation talk, I decided I was going back in. Up I got and in I went. It was even tougher — it started the same but quickly got so thick I couldn't move! I didn't know what to do. I was pushing and pulling but I was stuck. Slowly I scraped my way inch by inch along the edge of the cliffs.

As the day went on I got to another small beach. At this point, I put my pack down and went for a walk along it. I found a cave and popped out on the other side of the peninsula.

I was apprehensive about going back into the bush, because it just didn't look good. Eventually I put on my pack and committed to the bush rather than the coast.

I had been right. It wasn't good. It was so bad. Despite not wanting to carry on, I had no choice. I was moving about 500 metres an hour. My pack was catching on everything and my body was getting ripped to shreds. It was almost like every single branch was out to get me.

After stopping for some nuts, I had to slide down a massive hill. It was crazy steep and at the bottom I almost fell in a blowhole. I was hoping the other side of the valley would be more pleasant. But once again, it wasn't.

I cracked. I screamed. I yelled, then I wailed like a baby. My body was wrecked. My blisters hurt. My shins were so bruised. My hands were cut to shreds. I had been miserably pushing through scrub like this for the last four days.

I kind of lost my mind and just started walking uphill. Just up. Up up up! I needed to get away from the coast. I climbed for two hours until I was almost 300 metres up and I could see the most beautiful clearing in the world 100 metres away. I decided I was going to camp there, and somehow found the drive to push through the wall that I had hit.

An hour later, I had moved through the last of that section of scrub. Up ahead was the only really open spot I had seen all day. There, I met another obstacle — the wind. It was freaking insane. It was blowing about 70 knots. I couldn't even stand up properly. I was almost being blown backwards as I walked.

It was so windy I had to pitch my tent hard up behind a rock but it didn't matter — I had made it through another day. It was so amazing up there. The granite seemed to have exploded up out of the earth.

I had a freeze-dried meal for dinner, which was the best part of the day. Watching the sunset over the Gogs made me even more determined to get there.

I couldn't sleep because it was so incredibly windy. But I was feeling strangely good. This had been by far the hardest day of my entire life. I've never been in a situation that was as hugely demanding as that one. It was just next level. But I'd survived it. I hadn't wanted to carry on but I did. I still had the rest of the bloody island to go, though . . .

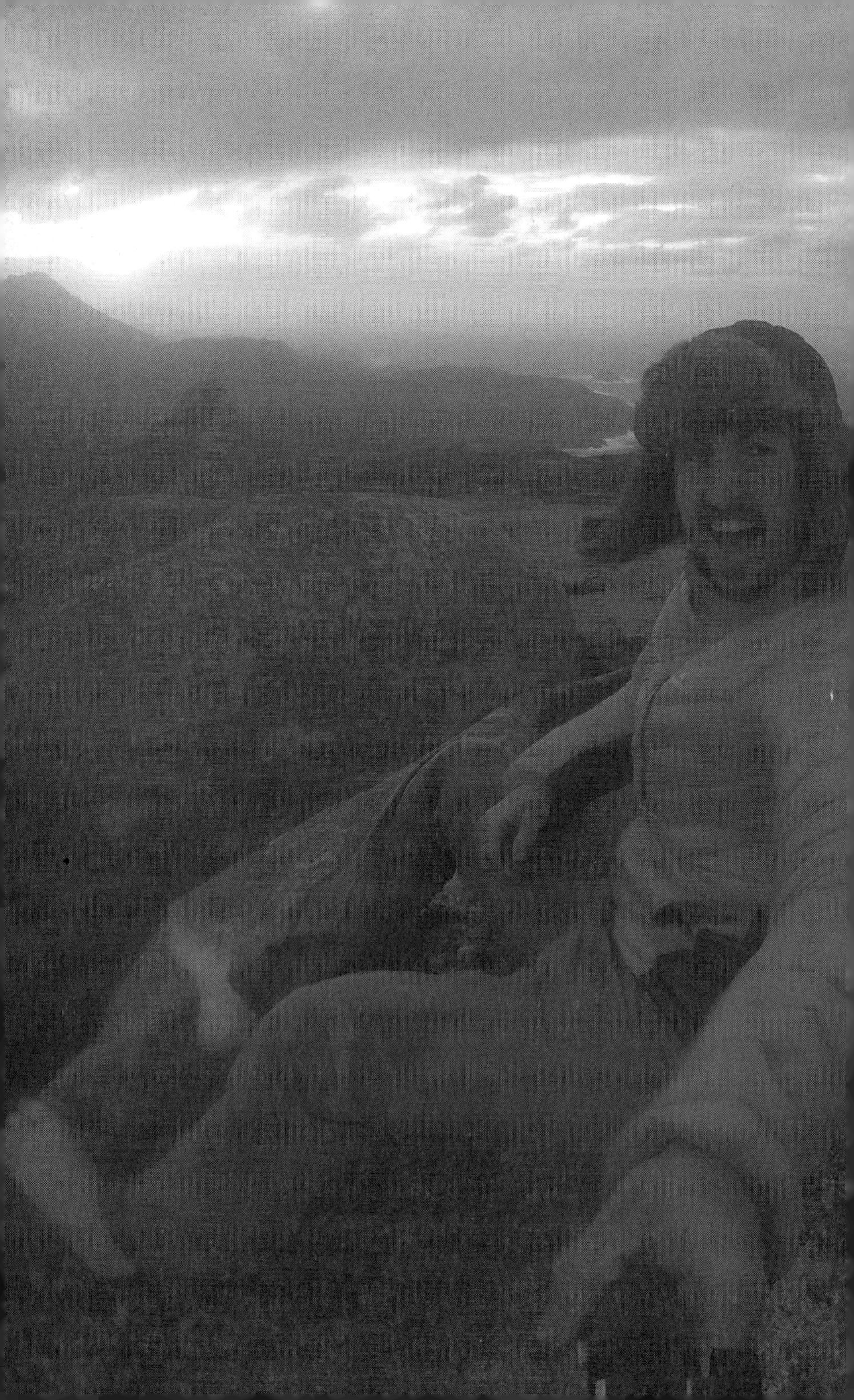

Chapter Six
TURNING POINT

> Day 14
> 23.11.16
> Just north of Magog to North Pegasus Hunters' Hut
> 13 km

Waking up in my tent, I felt busted and sore. My legs were bruised from the top of my thighs down to the end of my toes. My calves were really swollen and covered in cuts. My sores were all getting infected because they hadn't had a chance to dry out properly or be washed. My knees and my shins were completely smashed. Just packing my gear took a long time because my legs were so sore.

WHILE I SAT AND had breakfast, I got out my map. Inside it, I had a photo of my girlfriend, so every time I pulled it out I was reminded of how beautiful she is and how much I care about her. I kind of wished I had one of my family, too.

When you say to people who've come back from travelling, 'What was the coolest thing?', they always say the same line: 'It's the people you meet.' But I don't reckon it is. If you give yourself the chance to meet *yourself* then that is the coolest thing ever. That's what I was doing.

I was meeting myself — the real me — and discovering what that means, what it means to be human and live on the edge.

My plan for the day was to walk 1 kilometre and stop. Then I was going to put up my tent, leave my gear in it and climb up Magog.

My legs weren't too happy about the idea, but that climb had been my goal since not long after I started this trip. I decided that the climb would conclude my descent to the south, and after it I would head north. Yep, the decision I'd been battling with for so long had been made. I was no longer going to head further south, as I'd originally planned.

It was a hard decision to make, but I came to the conclusion that I was here for me and not for anything else. I had to do what made *me* happy — and the thought of days and days of more scrub-wrestling definitely didn't make me happy. I just didn't want to walk around the coast anymore because I hadn't seen anything other than the scrub. Every day looked exactly the same. I saw nothing but scrub.

If I went any further south I'd have to walk back that way too, whereas from here I could go into new territory that I didn't have to cross twice. I knew I was doing the right thing because it was going to be better for me in the long run.

I'm so glad I didn't commit to heading down to the south coast. It just changed the adventure so that it was something that I remember as being really fun. There didn't seem to be any change in the landscape coming so

I would have had just more of the same for days on end. There was no point in doing something I was really not enjoying just for an arbitrary goal. I didn't want to keep doing it just to say I'd done it. There was no real reason to carry on doing it just because that's what I said I'd do. I could change the plan because that's what worked for me. It didn't affect anyone but me ultimately.

I decided that I would spend the rest of my time having an adventure on the island — walking to different locations — still travelling a long distance but now I would actually have some fun.

On any adventure, the outcome is uncertain. Only you can change the outcome — so that's what I did.

After making the decision, I felt terrible for quite a while. I felt like I'd failed. Every step I took, I felt like I was a total failure. I felt like I'd failed myself and everyone else who was interested in what I was doing. I felt like I'd let a whole lot of people down.

But the fear and the sadness I had been feeling faded away. I started to feel excited about what I was going to do — and that's how I should have been feeling all along. The rain had stopped, the sun was shining and I was going to do some climbing in a ridiculously amazing place.

The landscape here was dominated by these huge granite outcrops. It was so beautiful. Some of them look like massive sculptures, where one big rock is sitting on top of other ones. They look like they should never be able to balance but somehow they do. There is nowhere else in New Zealand that looks like it.

The wind had died off quite a lot so I was looking

forward to climbing the Gogs. I had been able to see them getting closer and closer for days.

I headed down into the valley. The way down was insane. It was like a 75-degree slope covered in wet moss. If I had slipped, it would have been over. I would have tumbled down to the bottom and not got back up. I made my way down slowly and carefully.

When I got to near the base of Magog, I put all my stuff down, pulled out my solar panels and started charging everything. I didn't pitch my tent, though, as I thought I might be able to walk a bit further later in the day. I managed to just ace it with the timing for the day — the sun was out and I had plenty of time to do some climbing before I needed to head off to find a place to sleep for the night. I set off to climb Magog.

I slowly made my way up. I still had a bit of scrub to make my way through, but because it was only about chest height and quite dense I worked out a new way to get through it — or should I say over it: I pretty much body-surfed across the top of it. I climbed up, up, up until I hit a track. Someone had made a track up there! I followed it right the way to the very top of Magog.

The climb was 282 vertical metres, and it was very steep — especially the last bit that went almost straight up — but it was totally worth it. It was such a relief to climb without my pack and not to have to worry about getting smacked in the face by thousands of trees. Along the way, I stopped and drank from puddles that had formed in dips in the granite. That was the most delicious water I'd had in a while.

The view from the top was stunning. I'm so glad I went up there. Everything was so big and beautiful. I was even a little bit glad I was alone to experience it for the first time. Now I know where the most beautiful place in the world is.

I could see all the way back to Easy Harbour and quite a long way to the south. From what I could see, it looked like more of the same horrible scrub. Standing up there helped me to realise I'd made the right decision. It also helped me to work out the route I'd take for the rest of the day.

From the top of the mountain, I could see that there was a huge river valley running east. I decided I was going to follow it to the other end. On the map, I could see that it came out onto Cook Arm, which itself runs off the South Arm of Port Pegasus.

I climbed down because there was a storm rolling in and I needed to pack up my solar panels. I was a bit gutted I didn't climb the Gog, which is next to Magog and is even higher. I thought about doing it, but with the storm that was heading this way I decided it was just too risky. That turned out to be a good decision on my part.

THE RIVER VALLEY TURNED out to be swampy and there were heaps of little streams running through it, so I had wet boots for most of the day. It took a bit of navigating but it was totally worth it because it meant one thing and one thing only: No. More. Scrub. Yes!

The swamp reminded me of the scene in *The Lord of the*

Rings where there's a whole lot of dead people in a marsh — it was just like that, but without the dead people.

There were plenty of plants growing in the valley but they were all just little and I could easily walk around them or hop over them. There were also big, long patches of sandy mud with hardly any vegetation at all. It was so, so good to just be able to walk without having to find my way around or through any scrub.

I had planned to just walk a few kilometres then camp on the flats, but when I got to Cook Arm the tide was out. I quickly realised that I should make the most of it and keep walking. I was absolutely stuffed but I knew that if I pushed on, I might be able to make it to the hut at North Pegasus by nightfall.

Walking along the inlet at low tide was the most amazing thing I'd encountered in ages. It was flat. It was open. There was no scrub. That all made me very happy.

There were parts where I had to get into the water to get around rocky outcrops. I was up to my waist in freezing-cold water and I couldn't stop thinking about the fact there might be sharks in there. Apart from that, I was happy. I was even happier when I came across some rocks covered in mussels. Yes — mussels for dinner!

At the end of Cook Arm, I had to climb back into the bush for about a kilometre to get to the hut. The bush here was open and made for easy progress. As I made my way along, I almost stepped on a kiwi! It was right in front of me and I didn't even notice it. I got quite a shock as I saw it race off into the bush. Man, I love those kiwi. This had turned into a very good day.

The day only got better as I made my way down a steep little track to the North Pegasus Hunters' Hut. It was a good sight after a long, hard day. I was so happy to see the hut. I'd surprised myself by covering about 13 kilometres that day — as well as climbing Magog — and I was so ready to rest.

The hunters' huts are a bit more simple than the tramping huts but this one was more than enough for me. Someone had even left a pillow there! It was so exciting.

The view across the Pegasus Passage was beautiful. There were a couple of little islands and, in the distance, big old Anchorage Island. I could walk straight off the porch onto the beach. It was so peaceful and freaking fantastic.

Someone had left some noodles at the hut so I cooked them up with the mussels I'd harvested just half an hour beforehand. It was the perfect way to end a long, very tough day.

Day 15
24.11.16
North Pegasus Hunters' Hut (REST DAY!!!)

A DAY IN THE North Pegasus Hunters' Hut did me the world of good. I didn't want to move! I was so sore from the last few days of adventure. There was no dry wood and the rain wouldn't stop so I didn't manage to get the fire going. It was unfortunate, as I had hoped to wash my clothes but no fire meant no dry clothes. I did manage to get my BioLite going so I could have hot food, however. After I ate the noodles I found some spaghetti, and I ate that, too.

I made myself a nest in the corner of the room, chose some mags that had been left in the hut and started reading. Man, I wished I had a good book to read! I had left *On the Road* back at the last hut, to save weight.

After doing some reading and mapping I had a nap. It was the best nap ever! I woke up feeling great. My body was a little stiff and sore so I went for a small look around the rocks, hoping to find some easy dinner. I only found a huge sea snail but I didn't eat it.

Back at the hut I emptied out my bag and counted my meals. I had 22 days' worth of food left, plus about five days of nuts and some rice to mix with my dinners to make them a bit more bulky.

I could tell I had lost weight. I felt lighter and I was getting cold more easily. I was having to wear all my clothes so I didn't get too cold.

I had one of my freeze-dried meals for dinner. Just before I went to bed I made a cup of tea with my last tea bag. I was hoping it was going to be green tea or chamomile tea. It wasn't. It was gumboot tea. It made me so wide awake it wasn't even funny. I couldn't get to sleep for the life of me. I lay there with my eyes shut for hours.

Even though I couldn't sleep it had been a great day. I was heading north from then on.

> Day 16
> 25.11.16
> North Pegasus Hunters' Hut to start of the Tin Range Surveyors' Track
> 9 km

AFTER AN EPIC DAY of rest, I was up early to watch the sunrise out the front of the hut. The bay was so calm and the light was so peaceful.

Sitting outside the hut, with a pot of water boiling on the stove and the beach in the background, I had spaghetti for breakfast, which I was stoked about. I couldn't believe I had already been going for 15 days.

I decided I'd get on the road early. I was headed back north towards the Tin Range. My loose goal was to skirt around North Arm until I got to the base of the range. There was a track that headed up to the top of the range and I was keen to find it.

From the hut, I headed back across the hill to the end of Cook Arm and began making my way north. It felt good to be going in the direction of home. I kept my eyes out for the kiwi I spotted yesterday but unfortunately had no luck.

Once I got to the head of the Pegasus Passage, I stopped to look at my map to make sure I was going the right way. I followed some flattish hills that took me into Bens Bay. It seemed way too easy. I was there in about 20 minutes. I was quite impressed with my quick walking so I charged on. I got a bit carried away and was really annoyed that there seemed to be a small creek in every single gully when only the big ones are on the map. So when I thought I was at one place, actually I was nowhere near it. It screwed me up a few times. Finally, I reached the point that I had originally been aiming for, at the head of Albion Inlet. It took me only three hours.

From there I had to cross a small river and then pretty much head north. I set my compass and charged on up a 100-metre hill. The bush up there was so open and easy to walk through. It was bush that doesn't need thinking about. That's the best kind.

I spent most of the day just following my compass as I made my way through the bush. The walking was kind of easy, as when I was in the bush it was all fairly open and what scrub there was was much less densely packed and much easier to get through than what I had experienced further south. I was still bush-bashing a little bit but it had nothing on what I had been doing over on the west coast. The rain made an unwelcome return, but it was light and the wind was nowhere near as bad as it had been.

All that rain meant that the rivers were running quite high, so I had to be particularly careful when I was crossing them. Although I say rivers, most of them were probably usually just small streams but there'd been so much rain that they were really full. Sometimes I got lucky and there would be a fallen tree across the water which I could make my way across. But sometimes I had no choice but to wade.

There was one big river that I had to be super careful about crossing. It took me a while but eventually I found a shallow bit at the top of a little waterfall and slowly made my way across.

By early in the afternoon, the rain stopped and the sun came out. I was so happy to have a bit of sun on me and the light made the forest look way nicer, plus it helped dry my wet legs from wading through the water.

Even though I was feeling much happier and I was moving faster, I still found myself obsessing about food. As I walked I dreamed about having freshly baked apple pie, ice cream and hot vanilla custard. Then I thought about how much I missed pies. Who would have thought that meat, flour and butter all mixed together would be so damn nice, especially with a big dollop of tomato sauce right on the top!

In my head, I listed all the different types of food I wanted. Pizza was pretty high up the list. It was almost as if food would fill a void in me somehow — and not just the void in my empty stomach.

As I walked I made up a whole bunch of songs, sang bits of other songs, whistled at the birds and even danced for a little while. That wouldn't have been possible a couple of days ago. I just felt so much happier. Finally, I was having fun! I could barely take the smile off my face.

One of my songs went something like this:

I've been here in the bush, walking for weeks now.
I don't know how I got here, but it doesn't matter.
I'm just going to keep on walking.
Walking's what I do.
A bit of scrub-bashing tooooo.
All I really know is how to get through.
How to push my body through this,

Then fight them back too
Get the emotional days but the good ones too
That's why I love you.
I'm here in the bush
Nothing to do
So I pick up my camera and sing a little tune
I know I can't sing
But there's no one here to hear
See my little thing that I did there!

THEN I HIT a patch of scrub and the singing stopped. It was too hard to think and sing and bush-bash all at the same time. Luckily, it was only a small patch and it wasn't long till I popped out on the other side back into open bush.

Don't get me wrong, it was still hard going. I was still a few days away from being back on DOC tracks, and I still worried a bit about how much food I had with me, but now that I was having fun, everything felt like it was back in perspective. I was happy to be able to just walk wherever I wanted. I felt really happy that almost all of the island is a national park so I really could go wherever I liked.

While I was walking, I came to the conclusion that going downhill in scrub is way harder than going uphill. I'd had four days to think about it and compare the two situations. Going downhill on Stewart Island, the gravity and the mud help you along the way. When you mix gravity and mud, you get slipping over about fifty times a day. Going uphill, it's kind of the same with the mud and the slipping but it's way easier to control because you can use more muscles. Going downhill, you're really just using your feet and luck to try to stop the slipping.

After about six hours' walking, I could hear a waterfall and see a horizon. It was pretty exciting. I could tell from my map that I must be near Belltopper Falls. Apparently, it's called that because back in the day some dude lost his bell-top hat when it fell into the falls. I couldn't imagine anyone wearing a top hat down here!

The falls were huge and spectacular. I crossed them at the top where it looked like there was an old dam, or something manmade anyway — a relic of the past. I dropped my pack on the other side and headed down to the bottom to take in the full beauty of the falls. They were about 15 metres wide and made up of three different drops. All the rain we'd been having meant they were flowing really strongly and the power of them was awesome.

The spot where I wanted to camp wasn't far away. I could see it from the falls, but to get there I had to make my way around the coast.

Just beyond the falls, the water flowed out into one of the inlets of North Arm. I crossed the inlet and then carried on a few hundred metres uphill to my campsite for the night. It was a little way along the Tin Range Surveyors' Track, which hadn't been maintained since 2004. The first bit of the track was still solid, which was a good sign. I was sure I'd get lost a few times along the way but that was all part of the adventure.

There were a few bricks lying around — I think they

were from the old fish factory that used to be there — so I gathered them into a circle and lit a fire in it. I used a bendy bit of tree as a washing line and hung all my wet clothes over it. I even washed my shirt. I got the BioLite going to charge my phone and boil some water, which I used to cook a big feed of mussels that I'd gathered down at the inlet. They were delicious. I was a very happy camper. I had food, fresh water, clean clothes and a sheltered tent site.

After I'd eaten I went down to the inlet to see if I could get some paua. I felt like there was something in the water with me so I got out. Then I saw this massive sea lion. It swam around a bit and would come up for air and grunt at me. Eventually, it came up right close to the shore, looked straight at me for quite a while, and had a bit of a growl at me. Luckily, I was sitting on top of quite a high, steep bank that it couldn't have got up, otherwise I might have been in trouble. It was hands down the biggest sea lion I'd ever seen in my life. It was intimidating but very cool. I definitely wasn't going to try for paua again so got some more mussels instead.

I had started trying to dry my shirt when the rain started. I quickly put everything inside my tent and made sure it was done up. There were sandflies everywhere so I was itchy, but apart from that I was quite happy with life. In fact, I'd had an amazing day. It was one of the best days of the trip so far.

I was so content with what I was doing. I was just so happy in the space I was in. I had covered about 9 kilometres and I felt really free, just doing what I wanted to. I felt like I was just getting into it, just starting to remember why I was doing this. I was becoming free, becoming me. It was so nice, so liberating to just be myself.

✕

Crossing rivers

I'm always super careful when I cross rivers, especially after having a couple of freaky experiences when I was walking around New Zealand. The key things to do are find the safest spot to cross and also to be aware of when a river isn't safe to cross. Here are a few helpful hints I've learnt.

Don't ever cross if:
- ✕ You feel like the river is too swift.
- ✕ There is debris in the river.
- ✕ The river is brown and flooded.

If it is safe to cross, then:
- ✕ Go with the flow so you're not fighting the current.
- ✕ Make sure you are aware of your surroundings and check for hazards downstream.
- ✕ Cross at the widest part of the river as it is often the shallowest and slowest part.

It is always safest to cross a river as a group if you can. Link arms or put your arms behind each other's backs (between packs if you have them) and cross with the strongest people at the front and rear.

And always remember to put your gear in a waterproof pack liner — that way it'll stay dry if you fall in!

✕

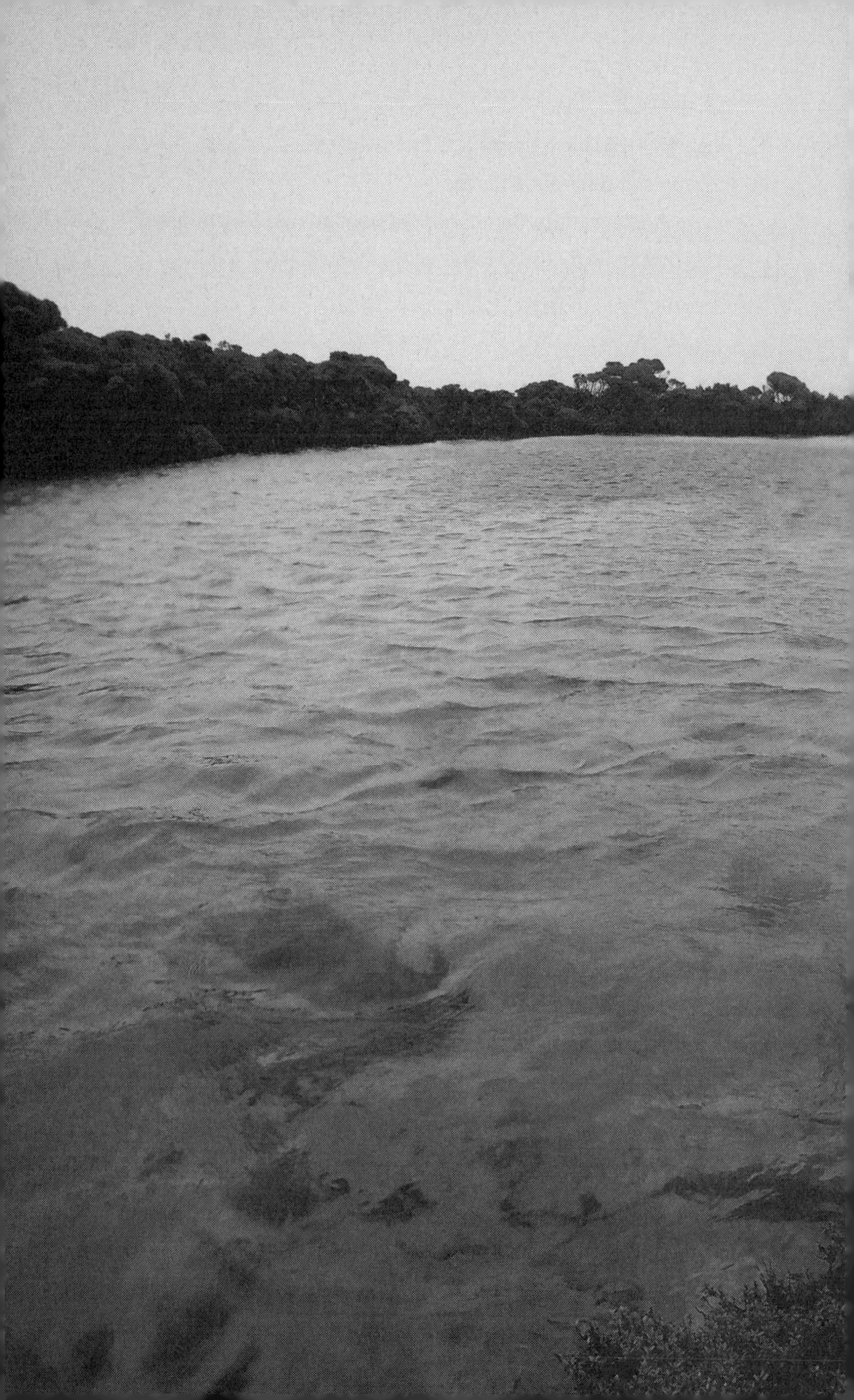

Chapter Seven

FACING DEATH

> Day 17
> 26.11.16
> Start of Tin Range Surveyors' Track to top of Tin Range
> 7 km

On the morning of day 17, I was still in my tent at 8.30 a.m. I should have been packing but outside there was a wild storm. It was windier than I had ever seen it in my whole life. I was not looking forward to going out there.

MY RAIN JACKET HAD stopped being a rain jacket, and was just a jacket now. I shouldn't have worn it in the scrub, but the scrub had been wet and I didn't want to be wet. Now the jacket had holes in it and let the rain in. Nothing against the jacket — nothing could have withstood going through that scrub.

I just sat there, in my sleeping bag, not wanting to go anywhere. I knew I was going to have to deal with the fact that I was going to get wet, I was going to get cold and there wasn't a thing that I could do about it. It's fair to say that I was a bit apprehensive about leaving that morning.

I eventually got going about 9.40. I skipped breakfast because I decided I was happy with a few handfuls of nuts. Today was going to be easy because I would be following a track.

However, the sign at the start of the track said: 'This

track is no longer maintained. It has been left to revert back to its natural state. Parts may be difficult to access or may no longer exist.'

For something that hadn't been maintained, it was pretty damn open. The lower parts of the track were absolutely fantastic. It made me realise how much I'd missed walking on tracks. I love the off-track stuff, but the on-track stuff was much easier and much more fun. Even though there'd been no maintenance for almost 13 years, the trees hadn't grown over the track. I couldn't get over how fantastic it was or how fast I could move on it.

I was happy with the progress that I was making but was aware of the strong winds that were bending the trees. There were moments of sunshine and I was thinking, 'Man, it would have sucked if I had taken the day off because of the weather . . .'

As the day wore on, the wind continued to pick up and the rain became more frequent. The higher I climbed, the colder I got. My lack of food meant I was becoming cold quickly — way quicker than normal.

About midday, I reached the top of the surveyors' track. From there I took the Tin Range Tramway. As its name suggests, there used to be trams running up and down it as part of a tin-mining operation. The tin had originally been discovered by gold miners who had come to the island in the 1880s.

The tram track was big and wide and easy to follow. It climbed up to about 400 metres before coming to a stop at the bottom of a hill where the old mine was located. From here on, I was going to follow what's known as the Tin Range route — but there was no track and no markers so I was pretty much on my own.

On the Tin Range, I came across a whole lot of old glass bottles stashed under a tree. They looked like they'd had a couple of litres of something very strong in them at some point. There were also some broken-down old sheds, some tram wheels and lots of other old industrial stuff.

It's hard to imagine what life must have been like for the miners up there. It must have been miserable.

I climbed up and up until I reached the bush line and the alpine scrub started. The wind really kicked in when I got up there. At first, I could deal with it. It was strong but I was fine. Slowly it got stronger and stronger. It started to make my throat sore and made it hard to breathe.

I thought that was odd, but I pushed on for about an hour being shoved around by the wind. I spent some time in the scrub when I lost the track. It was so thick, I couldn't believe I had walked through it for four days. Now I got sad/bad feelings just looking at it.

I carried on up towards the top of the range. It was quite flat up there but it was completely exposed. There was nothing much growing except tussock, a bit of speargrass, the odd mountain flax bush and some olearia. The rain had stopped but the wind was still getting worse. My happy mood from yesterday was quickly turned angry by the wind. I don't know why but wind sometimes just makes me really angry.

It was hard to try to stay upright walking through knee-high scrub. At one point, a gust was so strong that it blew me off my feet. It was crazy. To make it worse,

I was up high enough that I could see a storm coming, and with it there was going to be a lot of rain. I knew that I'd have no real way of sheltering from it. All I could do was keep moving.

Twenty minutes later I was walking along the ridge. The only positive thing about the wind was that it had dried my clothes. That's when the rain/hail/snow started falling and it wasn't just falling, it was being forced out of the skies by the crazy wind. It was coming at me sideways. And I was cold. Really cold.

I had never been in a situation like this one before. It was not nice. By this point, I was soaked. All my gear was borderline freezing and my hands . . . well, they didn't even work. At about two o'clock I found a little patch of low bush and sat down next to it.

I was huddled in a ball next to a bush in the rain. That's when I realised something was really wrong. I thought to myself, 'This is kind of weird. Why am I not still walking and keeping warm in the rain?' There was something wrong about me just sitting in a bush but I couldn't work out what it was. Then I realised. It was like 'Woah! I'm really, really cold!' I was so cold that I'd stopped shivering.

At that moment, the rain stopped and I started walking again to try to warm up. I kept moving for another 15 minutes or so, then the rain and hail started. The hail was heavy, smashing into any exposed skin. I was on the brink of being so cold that I wasn't *feeling* cold anymore. I was aware that I had hypothermia and that I needed to do something right now. If I didn't, I was going to die.

The wind sent chills through my body. I couldn't keep

going — I just wanted to sleep. I huddled behind some scrub, desperately trying to find some shelter. It was looking bad at this point. I had to do something straight away. I decided I needed to pull the plug for today. I knew I'd made a dumb move coming up here and that the only thing to do was to try to find somewhere flat where I could set up camp and try to wait out the storm.

I found the first place out of the bad wind and went into full survival mode. I pulled out my tent, and started putting it up next to a big flax bush. The hail and rain were relentless, filling the inside of my tent very fast. The rain was so heavy that there was at least a litre of it in there before I managed to get my fly on. I was growling at myself. How could I be so stupid? Everything was getting wet and I wasn't thinking properly.

There was nothing to pin the tent to and I ended up tying it to random stuff and just knotting it. I just hoped like hell it would stay standing. As soon as it was up, I jumped inside and used my pot to bail out the water. I used my towel to soak up the leftovers and squeezed it out outside. It was just blowing like I'd never heard before.

I was wet, cold and shivering uncontrollably (this was good as it meant my body was warming up a little). My fingers were so numb. I fumbled as I attempted to take off my soaking-wet rain jacket. Once I'd managed to get it off, I took off my other wet clothes, then, as quickly as I could, I put on every other piece of dry clothing I had. My teeth chattered as I did it. I had to get as warm as I could, and fast.

I unwrapped my survival bag and climbed into it. I

inflated my sleeping mat to keep me a bit further off the freezing ground. Then I unrolled my sleeping bag and stuffed myself and the survival bag into it. I put my hat on and did it up real tight, then I snuggled as far as I could into my sleeping bag.

I had never been that cold in my whole life. It was totally terrifying. It was only three in the afternoon but I knew that this was my only hope of survival. It was one of the scariest moments I had ever experienced.

A hot meal would have helped warm me up but because I only had a wood-burning cooker I couldn't get the fire lit, so I had to have a cold meal. I ate that and went to sleep. I was so exhausted.

Once I started to warm up I knew that I was going to be all right, but if I hadn't made the decision to stop right there and then, I don't know what would have happened. There was nowhere else up there that I could have pitched my tent and I don't know if I would have been able to even if I'd wanted to.

On reflection, my mistake was leaving my original campsite. I had woken up with a bad feeling. I should have listened to my instincts but I didn't.

While I was lying huddled in the tent, I realised that I could have died up there. I don't think I'd ever been so close to death before. I recorded two videos — one for my parents and my sister, and one for Ngaio — just in case anything else happened.

VIDEO FOR NGAIO:

Hey Ngaio, I'm just recording this, not that I think

anything's going to happen but just in case. I want you to know that you are the most important person in my life. I couldn't have done what I did or been who I am today without your help. You're my light. You're my rock. I love you so, so much and I'm sorry. I love you. You're so amazing. The most amazing person in the entire world.

VIDEO FOR MY FAMILY:
Hey Mum, Dad and Brooke, I just wanted you guys to all know that I really love you and I'm sorry. I'm sorry for this. Other than that, thank you for the most amazing life anyone could have ever had. I know I struggled throughout my whole time. I'm not sure if . . . I'm not sure . . . I love you guys so much. You're so important to me in so many ways. I didn't appreciate you the way that I should and I'm sorry for that. Family is one of the most important things ever. I just want you guys to know that I love you so much. I couldn't be who I am today without you so thank you. I love you.

I ALSO WROTE a note in my diary.
I've never been so cold. I'm not sure I'm going to survive. Just in case this is the last thing I ever write, I want everybody to know how much I love them. This is my last hurrah. I enjoyed it all so much. Thanks for being the best. You have all been so great to me. I love you all so much.

THANKFULLY, THAT DAY'S WEATHER didn't lead to any of my loved ones having to watch those videos or read that last message from me. Five hours later, at about 8.30 p.m., the storm had blown itself out.

I unzipped the tent to see blue sky and a slowly setting sun. The scene couldn't have been more different than it had been earlier. At least there was something beautiful about the end of my day, I guess.

I hung all my clothes on a line in the tent in the hope that they would be dry the next morning. I knew it probably wouldn't work but it was better than leaving them in a wet pile in the corner.

Even after the storm had blown through, the whole tent was heaving in the wind. I couldn't believe how a day that had been so easy at first had turned into the worst day ever. I really needed to get some sleep so I had enough energy to get down from here the next day. But I was a little bit scared to fall asleep because of how windy it still was and because of just how close I had been to dying.

✕

Hypothermia

I found out first-hand just how scary hypothermia can be. Luckily, I recognised what was going on and did something about it straight away.

Basically, hypothermia occurs when your body loses more heat than it can produce. Being wet or in cold wind will always make this worse, as both of those things lower your body temperature.

The most important things to know about hypothermia are the warning signs and what to do if you're getting it.

The warning signs are (in order of seriousness):

- Shivering, which is your muscles trying to generate their own heat.
- Irritability, being a bit unco and then your speech starting to slur, as your brain starts losing a bit of power.
- Getting really tired, as your body begins to shut down. (I reckon I was at this point when I finally stopped and put up my tent.)
- Getting really irrational and argumentative usually comes next, along with not being able to stand up.
- Then the body shuts down all but the most necessary functions, so when people are found in this state it looks like they're dead. Next stop is actually being dead.

Treating hypothermia can be tricky, depending on what stage you are at. The thing to remember is not to heat your body externally, because this can cause more damage. The most important thing is to reduce further heat loss, and let your body warm itself. Here's how to do that:

- Get out of the cold — put up your tent, hide in a windbreak or any other kind of shelter you can find.
- Get out of any wet clothing and put on dry stuff if you've got it.
- If you can stand, do a little bit of exercise to warm yourself up.

- ✕ If you can't stand, get into your sleeping bag, then put that into your survival bag (not the other way round like I did, because I woke up all wet!).
- ✕ Put a sleeping mat or any other dry stuff between your sleeping bag and the ground to insulate you from it.
- ✕ Put on a hat, or wrap something around your head to keep it warm.
- ✕ Eat some food — an energy bar or something sugary — and have something to drink. Water is good, or small sips of a warm drink, like tea or hot chocolate.

There are some things you definitely shouldn't do:

- ✕ Don't drink alcohol. You might momentarily feel warm but it will dull your reactions, and no one needs that when things are getting a bit dangerous.
- ✕ Don't rub or massage your skin, as your blood flow will be a bit stuffed and it could cause damage.
- ✕ Most of all, don't sit by a fire or a heater. This can send cold blood to your heart and lungs and that is what you're trying to avoid.

A person with severe hypothermia is in danger of heart failure. If you're wondering whether or not to set off an emergency beacon or call an ambulance, the answer is 'yes!'

✕

> Day 18
> 27.11.16
> Top of Tin Range to halfway down Tin Range
> 18 km

DURING THE NIGHT, I spent a lot of time thinking about my planned route. My original thought had been to head north to the top of Blaikies Hill and then east into the bush across to Toitoi Flat and up to South West Arm on Paterson Inlet. But I decided against that, as I knew I needed to get to the nearest hut — Rakeahua on the Southern Circuit track — so I could get everything dry and spend some time resting and recovering. It was about two days' walk away. From there, I decided I was just going to have a good adventure. I was going to have some fun and do what was right by me.

I had had a horrible night's sleep. I was way too cold and my sleeping bag was really damp because I had stuffed my survival blanket inside it. That just made me wet. It was so wet that I thought I'd peed myself! That's how much moisture was in the bag.

I lay there feeling scared for my life, knowing that I had to go out into bad weather in wet clothes. Wet weather and being on the tops was a dangerous combination. I was on a mission to get as far down the mountain as I could before 1 p.m., when even worse weather was due to hit.

As I unzipped the tent at about 6.30 a.m., I was greeted by a large pile of unmelted hail. No wonder it was so friggin' cold up there! I could see my breath. I managed to light some flammable goo (that I'd been carrying as back-up fuel) in the BioLite. It burned fast and hot but

I lay there feeling scared for my life, knowing that I had to go out into bad weather in wet clothes. Wet weather and being on the tops was a dangerous combination.

I managed to heat some water. (With all the ice lying around, I didn't have to go far to get fresh water!) I was super happy to have a hot meal of freeze-dried venison casserole before I headed out into the cold. Having some calories to burn warmed me up for a bit.

I was worried about what the day was going to bring, and I knew that while I had warmed up, I wasn't out of trouble just yet. It's easy for hypothermia to reoccur if you don't eat properly. My rain jacket was full of holes from the scrub so I didn't have anything to keep the water off me. I decided to cut up my survival bag and wear that as a base layer. My whole body was then wrapped in an unbreathable bag so it was a bit sweaty but at least it kept the rain off.

I didn't really know whether I'd be able to make the distance down off the tops in those conditions with the gear that I had. I definitely didn't bring the right gear for alpine conditions. Snow was not on my list of things to look out for — not on the coast, anyway. But once I changed my plans and went inland, a whole new field of terrain and weather had opened up.

Once I'd eaten and had all my gear on, I headed out into the cold at about 7.30 a.m. The sooner I got going, the sooner I'd be down off these freezing, windy hills. As I set off, it was still really windy but the sun was shining and there was blue sky. I was so happy to see it but I knew that it might not last long.

I had a big day ahead of me as I knew I had to traverse four peaks — Granite Knob (575 metres), Mount Allen (750 metres), Blaikies Hill (703 metres) and Table Hill

Me and my pack, Stewart Little — all geared up for the mission.

The cosy flight to Stewart Island.

Me and my buddies from Halfmoon Bay School.

The start of a long, long road.

I did go chasing waterfalls.

On a clear day, Stewart Island really does take some beating — pure natural magic.

Beautiful, but so cold!

My safe place.

Home sweet home.

Happy birthday to me! (With celebratory damper.)

Best paua of my life!

It doesn't look like much but this cave was an absolute luxury.

More than once, this trip pushed me to the very edge.

Sometimes, there seemed to be no way out.

Down time prompted a lot of reflection...

...as did the loneliness.

I missed my Wildgirl so much more than I could have foreseen.

The most meaningful achievements come from great challenges.

(716 metres) — before I could make it down to a lower part of the island.

The first mountain I got to was Granite Knob, and that was epic. It was massive. But looming behind it was Mount Allen, Stewart Island's second highest peak after Mount Anglem. As I walked, I could see it ahead of me — and right alongside it was an incoming hailstorm. It didn't take long to reach me and I was soon being pelted by little bullets of ice. Great. At least I felt a bit warmer from being wrapped up in my survival bag.

At the top of Mount Allen, I stopped to take some photos. I instantly got really cold. I figured that from the summit, I'd have a clear view north towards Blaikies Hill. I thought wrong. Just as I got to the top, the fog came rolling in. I couldn't see much at all. It was back to using my compass to work out where I was going. It became a navigational nightmare, trying to find my way through this mountainous range. There were so many spurs going off left and right that it was easy to get lost.

I spent the next few hours in the craziest fog ever, with the cold wind stinging my face. It was blowing sideways and freezing cold. I thought back to the previous day and started to get worried about hypothermia.

With Mount Allen ticked off, I headed downhill. As I went, I watched the wind blowing the fog away. It was so cool to watch the fog slowly being pushed away. It looked almost like smoke coming off the hilltops. The weather here can change so fast — as quickly as the fog got blown away, rain clouds floated in and it started to rain again. I sheltered briefly under some bushes while the worst of it passed through, then set off again.

Within about 20 minutes, the visibility was almost at zero again. I walked down a little bit onto the eastern side of the range and found there was barely any wind here, even though it was blowing about 40 knots on the other side. The price for being in the lee of the hill was terrible visibility, but I got out my compass and my map and I was good to go. I knew I'd be OK until I got to the other side of Table Hill, which was really steep and I'd need to be careful coming down off it.

I only had a few hours to go until I was off the ridge and out of the crappy weather so I pushed on over Table Hill. It was still blowing like anything up there and the climb was so tough that the only way I could keep moving forward was to count 'One, two, one, two, one, two . . .' in my head with each step.

I made it to the top of Table Hill at about 12.30. The top of the hill was covered in shallow puddles — I joked to myself that it was called Table Hill because of the water table. As I stomped across the flat, wet top of the hill, I was soaking and it was still super windy. And there was worse to come. I was fighting to stay warm and I knew that I had to keep moving, before even worse weather came. I didn't know if I'd be able to survive another night up here in my tent so I needed to get down off the hill — and fast.

The hail started coming again, along with sleet and some snow. I began to get really cold once again. I kept telling myself 'just a little bit further, a little bit further, push, push, you're just about off the mountain', but I was so bloody cold.

As I made my way down off the hill, I started to wonder if the cold had made me hallucinate. I thought I saw a person. *I did see a person!* They were far below me on the hill, but I could make out their bright orange jacket. I was suddenly filled with this new energy, this new excitement. I started running down the hill. I ran towards them as fast as I could — it took me about seven minutes to make it down to whoever this unsuspecting person was. It was 12.55 p.m. The worst of the storm was due any minute and, finally, I wasn't alone out here.

I can't describe the feeling. I hadn't seen anyone for about six days so it was really exciting to see another human. Until I saw him, I hadn't really wanted to see anyone, but when I saw him I suddenly remembered about people — and food.

From underneath a tightly pulled orange hood, a big smile beamed at me. 'What are you doing up here?' he asked.

I could barely speak. 'I thought I'd drop down to the hut tonight. I can't see anything up here.'

Having removed his hood, I realised it was Mike from DOC, who I'd met a couple of weeks earlier at Mason Bay! I couldn't believe my luck. It barely seemed possible that out here in the middle of nowhere, with no tracks to follow, I would run into probably the only other person for miles — and I knew him.

He grinned and said, 'I've got a biv. If you want to stay with me, you're welcome.'

I thought, 'Bugger staying in a bivvy!' At that point, my brain had slowed down so much that I thought he meant his bivvy bag. That would have just been weird.

'Oh, naaa, it's all right. Everything's soaking wet. I need to get it dry before I head off,' I said. What was I thinking?

He must have known what I was thinking because he said, 'It's just like a hut. It's just through there.' He pointed into the fog.

I was a bit confused. 'The biv's just through there?'

'Yeah,' he replied. 'The hut's still quite far away. It's at least two and a half hours, depending on how fast you walk.'

'Oh, if it's just through there then, hell yeah, I'll stay. I thought you might have put it up somewhere higher up, and it's so windy.'

Mike said he still had quite a bit of work to do but that I could dump my stuff on the hillside and help him set his traps. He reckoned the bivvy was only 20 minutes away and that it was pretty big.

I asked if it was OK if I could just go and wait in the bivvy as I was totally freezing. He agreed immediately and gave me the co-ordinates for the bivvy. He then gave me a detailed explanation of various landmarks while I marked it on my map. Eventually, after he got halfway through describing the route to me, he decided it would be easier to just take me there himself.

I think he realised that I was in trouble so he walked me back to his bivvy. Even though I had the survival bag on, I was still really cold. I think it was because I didn't have enough food. The only thing that helped me get through that day was the fact I was wearing my survival bag. I'd never used one of them in my whole life. If I'm honest, I didn't think I'd ever be in a situation where I'd need one. That day I did. And it probably saved my life. I guess that's why they call them survival bags!

As we walked, I ramblingly told Mike what had happened the night before, then I talked non-stop about what I'd been through over the last couple of weeks. He told me later that I hadn't been making much sense. I was talking a lot of gibberish. I know I was happy to have someone to talk to for the first time in over a week, but now I think about it, I reckon my rambling had a bit more to do with the fact I was in the early stages of hypothermia again. I don't know what kind of state I would have been in if I'd had to walk another couple of hours down to the hut in that condition.

When we got to the bivvy, which turned out to be more substantial than I'd imagined, Mike made me a warm Milo. Faaaar out, Milo is so good when you are cold and tired! It was awesome. He then went back to work, leaving me sitting in the bivvy. He'd cooked some beans and sausages the night before and said I could help myself to them. Wow, that was even better than the Milo.

I was so happy to be dry and safe. I even found a pair of slippers. I lost my shit when I put my feet in them! They were so soft and squishy, they were the best thing I had worn in ages. The bivvy was basically a tricked-out hut with cool stuff in it for DOC workers. There was, like, a year's worth of food in there — maybe not a year, but it felt like it to me at the time!

Mike would base himself there for four days a week

and from there he'd go and set and check traplines for feral cats. There was a mountain dotterel breeding ground nearby, and also a population of harlequin geckos. DOC are working hard to protect both species so they trap pests and monitor the area quite closely.

A couple of hours later, Mike came back and cooked up this big tuna pasta bake. It was awesome! It felt like a tiny escape from the world I'd put myself in. We spent the night relaxing, chilling out, talking about adventures and drinking Milo. We talked about music. Then listened to music. It was so nice to hear music again.

It was a bloody awesome end to a pretty scary couple of days. By the time I'd warmed up, eaten and spent some more time talking to Mike, I went to sleep with a hot-water bottle *and* a blanket, feeling stoked with life once again.

The Tin Range

When I was camping at the bottom of the Tin Range, it was hard to imagine anybody living there. It's so isolated and such a wild place. Miners first went there in 1888 looking for gold, but they didn't find much. What there was, though, was tin.

The first rush for it only lasted a couple of years, but between 1912 and 1917, another lot of people came over to the island to have another go at mining the metal. They didn't get much tin out, but they did build a 7-kilometre-long tramway, which I walked along. There used to be a hotel and a post office up there as well, apparently.

Life was so tough for the tin miners that when drinking alcohol was prohibited on the rest of the island in the early 1900s, Pegasus Bay was the only place where it remained legal. I reckon those old fellas would have needed a drink to survive living and working down there.

More recently than that, a factory was built nearby to process fish caught in the area. Apparently, its refrigerators were run on kerosene — imagine the smell of that! It closed down in the 1950s and you can still see the remains of it at the bottom of the Tin Range Track.

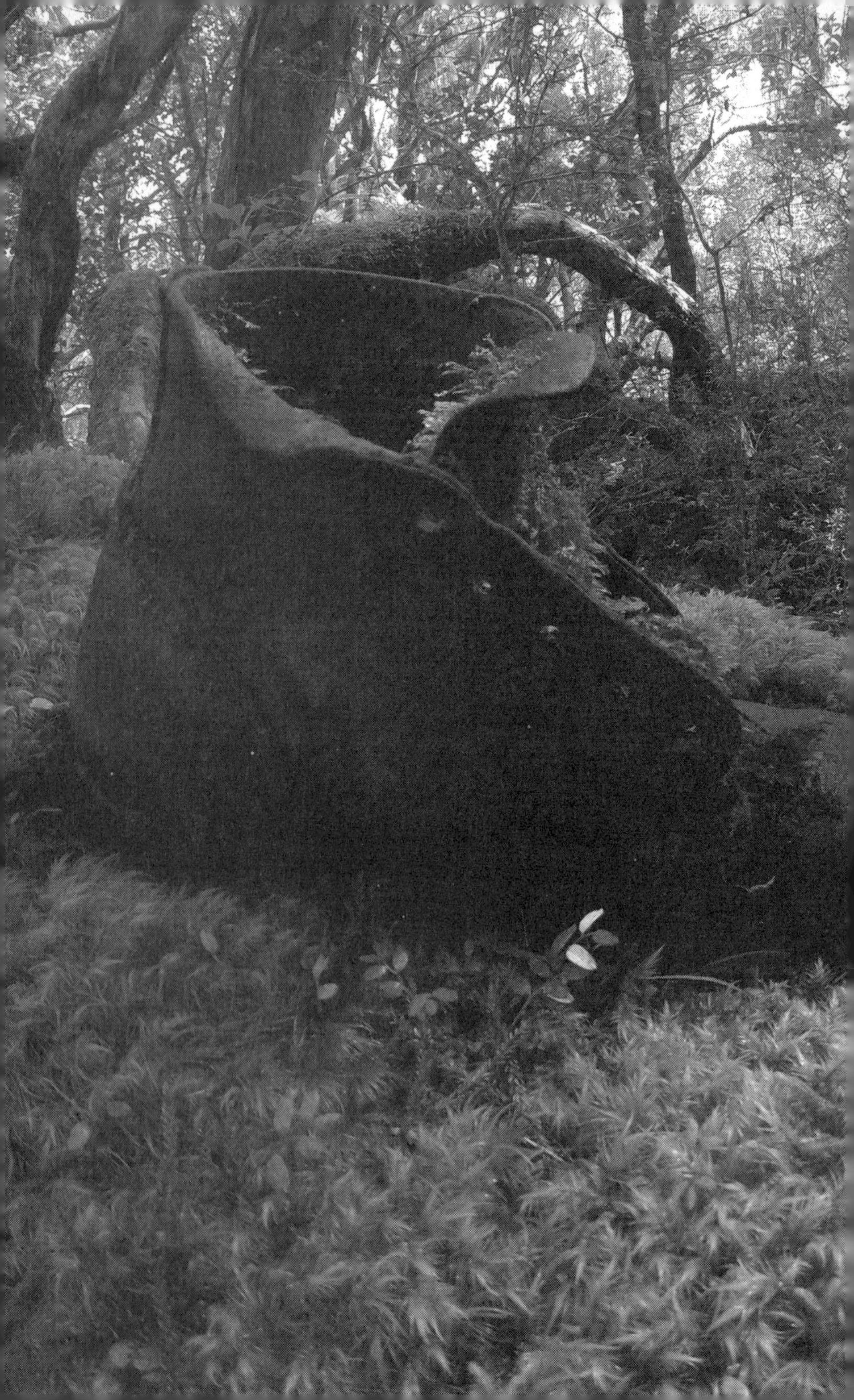

Chapter Eight
RELIEF

Day 19
28.11.16
DOC bivvy to Rakeahua Hut
9 km

After a great night with Mike in the bivvy, I packed up my gear and decided to have a short day walking just a couple of hours down to the Rakeahua Hut. It's at the base of Mount Rakeahua, which I was going to climb the next day on my 'rest' day. It's always good to keep moving, even when you're resting.

I WASN'T SURE WHERE I was headed after the hut. The route I had planned would have kept me on the tops for the next four days, but there was no way I could deal with another situation like what I'd just experienced. It was too close for comfort, really. This adventure wasn't worth my life. What it did make me realise though was that it was time to stop with all the misery and just start having fun. I love pushing my body to its limits but once you reach the limits, it isn't actually fun at all.

I had cellphone reception at the bivvy so managed to make a couple of phone calls. It was really nice to talk to Ngaio and my dad. That made my day a million times better.

I set off at about 8.30 a.m., feeling a bit apprehensive

about the fact that it was still raining. It had been hailing all night and after the last few days of cold weather, I was still a bit nervous. All my gear had been wet for weeks now and it wasn't nice putting on damp gear.

The bivvy was above the bush line — at about 580 metres elevation — so my day started out in the open, exposed to the same freezing wind that I'd finished in yesterday. It didn't take long before I could see a big storm racing up to meet me so I was happy that I didn't have to go far.

I was freezing for the first 20 minutes and then I warmed up and was fine. The tops were still as windy as anything. I just really wanted to get off them. I jumped onto the first sign of a track I could and started the huge descent to sea level. It was so slippery and wet, I fell over about every 10 steps. It makes me feel so clumsy when I can't even walk down a track properly. I slipped and slid my way down. The track was getting muddier and really boggy.

I might have almost died of hypothermia up on the tops, but I hadn't missed the mud. Some of the mud patches were so deep they came up to my thighs. The energy it took just to keep moving forward was insane. The previous day's storm also meant that all the little creeks were running really high, so it didn't take long before I was soaking wet.

The lower down I got, the more bush there was and the more sheltered from the wind I was. Once I was below the bush line, I could see the tops of the trees above me swaying in the wind but I was protected from it. I was still about 100 metres above sea level and the ground underfoot was really slippery but at least I was reasonably warm. There were a few really beautiful sections of the track that opened up to flats, and even though they were wet they were cool to walk through.

At one point in the bush, I came across a single, solitary old boot sitting on a rock. It had obviously been there quite a while as there was moss growing inside it. I thought for a bit about who it might have belonged to and why they'd left it there. The big hole in the toe of it might have had something to do with why it was abandoned but I'll never know. Thankfully, my boots were faring a whole lot better than that one. They'd been wet for pretty much 19 days and they'd held up really well.

Just before midday, I came across the welcome sight of a green and yellow DOC sign: 'This track is no longer maintained. It has been left to revert to its natural state.' The Tin Range was finished and I'd survived it — just.

I was back on the Southern Circuit track — for now, anyway. It felt like a lifetime since I'd left it at Doughboy Bay. It was a relief not to worry about getting lost or stuck in scrub anymore.

I walked along the first part, then it got ridiculously muddy. I have never seen mud like it. It was so deep that at one point I was up to my *waist* trying to pull myself out. It was so crazy. Thankfully, I only had about 2 kilometres until I reached the hut.

I was so happy when I got there. That little green hut meant that I had my first chance to wash my clothes in ages. I lit the fire, filled the metal ash bucket with water and heated it up. In went some of my dirty clothes and the previously clean, clear water quickly turned black from the collected sweat, mud and yucky stuff. While my clothes were soaking, I cooked up one of my freeze-dried meals and added a bit of rice to it to bulk it up. It was so nice to be inside while the rain started to fall again outside.

Once I'd hung up all my clean clothes to dry, it was time to give myself the same treatment. I filled the bucket with water again and set it on the stove to heat. It had been 14 days since I'd had a proper wash and I absolutely stank. It was pretty rank.

I took the bucket of hot water out onto the porch and stripped off. I tipped panloads of steaming water over myself and it was, hands down, the best feeling in the world. I was so happy to be clean and warm!

I chopped some firewood then started to make dinner for myself. I put a big dollop of coconut oil in a pan on the stove, so I could fry up some onion and garlic that Mike had given me. The only problem was I had lost my knife in the scrub way back on the west coast. There was only one thing for it — I bit off big chunks of raw onion and chucked them into the hot oil. It was a good thing that I was going to be the only one eating tonight! Then I got a clove of garlic, which I wasn't keen on using the bite technique to prepare. Instead, I bashed it against the bench, then ripped it into the pan as well.

While I was prepping the pan inside, I had a pot of rice cooking on my BioLite outside. Once it was done, I added it to the onion and garlic, to make a kind of pale-looking risotto. To all of this I added a packet of freeze-dried butter chicken. Candlelit dinner for one! Creamy, tomatoey, chickeny, ricey, oniony goodness. It was fricking delicious. I wished there were ten helpings of it, though!

After dinner, I looked at my maps and started trying to figure out what to do. Now I was back on a track, I had to decide whether to go off-track again and back into the 'not fun' zone once I'd had a rest. Or I could get a kayak and go back to that same 'not fun' zone by sea — which actually would be fun — then hike in from where I landed. To me, that seemed like a way better idea, because the coastline here is pretty much impossible to walk. With a kayak I could check out all the bays and waterways on Paterson Inlet, and maybe even head down to Port Adventure and Lords River on the eastern side of the island.

It was tricky, though, because I didn't know how I'd get a kayak. I tried to work it out but my brain was too kafuzzled. I figured the most important thing to do for now was to recover from all the bad days I had had then get back into it. I was in need of sleep and lots of food. Tomorrow would be a rest day — of sorts.

> Day 20
> 29.11.16
> Rakeahua Hut (rest day)
> 9 km (hike to the top of a mountain)

MY REST DAY WAS GOOD — but it wasn't really a rest day. I woke up at 8.30 a.m., after a wonderful night's sleep in a warm hut, to a sunny morning. Having had plenty of food and lots of sleep, my mental state had improved massively.

I was stoked about having dry clothes to put on, too. They were crisp and dry and they smelled delicious. After a big breakfast of freeze-dried Bolognaise, I decided to head up Mount Rakeahua. It was about 4.5 kilometres from the hut and involved climbing to 681 metres above sea level.

I left the hut at 9 a.m. I decided not to put my gaiters on over my boots because I thought it wouldn't be muddy. And what do you know? It was freakin' muddy. Right from the start of the track was deep mud. It was unavoidable — I just had to work my way through it. It was bloody enjoyable walking without a 30-kilogram pack on my back, though. I virtually ran along the track. It was fun: actual, proper, enjoyable fun.

It took me 45 minutes to get up to a beautiful tarn, where I stopped for a refreshing drink of mountain water. Once I got out of the bush, the route to the top was marked with sticks, which was a good thing as a bit of mist had started to roll in. It didn't look like I was going to get the epic view from the top that I'd been hoping for.

The weather slowly worsened and, in typical Stewart

The weather slowly worsened and, in typical Stewart Island summer fashion, it started to rain and hail.

Island summer fashion, it started to rain and hail. I pushed on, thankful that my freshly cleaned jacket was keeping me drier than it did when it was caked with mud, but slowly my clothes became wet again.

The further I went up the colder it got. I took shelter behind a small building that housed the solar panels used to power the radio tower at the top of the mountain. It was completely misty below me and the freezing-cold wind was absolutely blasting.

However, the altitude meant that I had cellphone coverage. I turned my phone on and made a call to my lovely girlfriend, Ngaio. It was so great to hear her voice — I was smiling from ear to ear. My plans had changed a lot so it was good to be able to let her and my family know what I was planning on doing.

I got hold of my dad as well, and discussed the possibility of getting a kayak to explore the coast with. As well as being able to get around more easily, it would be good for fishing, too.

Talking to Dad and Ngaio gave me an extra burst of energy, and I found myself running happily down the mountain, jumping over puddles as I went. I ran until I tripped over and landed on my face. That hurt!

I was hoping to meet Mike at the bottom of the hill before he headed back to base. I was keeping my fingers crossed that he might have had a block of cheese or something for me — something that was perishable that he couldn't just leave in the free-food box in the hut. When I got down, I'd missed him by about 10 minutes. I was gutted!

As I walked along the river valley back towards the hut, I heard the sound of an engine. I looked down towards the river and saw a boat with an outboard motor come flying past. The guy driving it waved as he shot past. It was DOC worker Dan, who turned out to be my new friend for the night. I offered to help him with his gear and I could see he had a gun, which made me hopeful that he was going to shoot a deer and I might get some meat.

Sure enough, not long after we got back to the hut, Dan left to do some hunting. Before he went he gave me a banana. It was the best thing I'd eaten in ages. It was so delicious and sweet.

I spent the rest of the afternoon hanging out at the hut. I'll let you in on a secret, though — I would get quite bored when I was staying in those huts by myself. I was so used to being out doing stuff that being surrounded by four walls with nothing much to do soon drove me a bit nuts. Thankfully, I had a notepad with me that I'd record each day's adventures on, just for something to do!

Staying in the same hut for more than a day also made me want to eat all my food. I cooked up some rice and chucked it in with a freeze-dried venison casserole sachet. My belly was well and truly full and I was very happy about that.

Later, I decided I needed to have a second dinner, so I cooked up some more rice and then fried it with some vegetables, which was delicious. I decided that it was all part of my recovery plan — more food equalled quicker recovery. I was craving chocolate and ice cream and apple pie and donuts and dumplings, though.

At about 9.30 p.m., I heard a loud *bang* about a kilometre away. I knew it was Dan's gun going off. I really hoped that meant he'd got a deer, which meant I might get some venison. I tried not to get too excited, as I'd have been disappointed if he didn't come back with anything.

He came back about an hour later with a nice big white-tail deer. He reckoned he couldn't initially tell whether he'd shot it or not, as it had taken him about 10 minutes to find the fallen animal. He reckoned he'd destroyed one of the lungs and the liver, but there was one thing he didn't damage, and he gave it to me as a present. The heart!

I could barely contain myself as Dan went to hang the deer in the woodshed overnight. Venison heart is one of my favourite foods in the whole world. I was so excited. Dan and I talked for a while before I headed off to bed.

At the end of my rest day, I was feeling pretty good. I'd been on an awesome walk up the mountain, my gear had dried in the hut, my sleeping bag was warm and I had finally started to have fun. Plus I had a deer heart to eat the next day.

Hunting on conservation land

Dan, who shot the deer and gave me the heart, is a DOC ranger. He knows the rules when it comes to hunting on the island, and especially on conservation land. They are:

- Hunting on public conservation land is not permitted during the hours of darkness (half an hour after sunset to half an hour before sunrise).
- Do not load a firearm in or near a hut — wait until you're hunting.
- Do not discharge firearms in the vicinity of huts, tracks, campsites, road ends or any other public place in a manner that endangers property or endangers, frightens or annoys members of the public.
- Do not load or discharge firearms within 500 metres of a Great Walk hut.
- When in a hut or camp, ensure you remove and store your firearm's bolt and ammunition separately. Where practical, also secure your firearm.

(Source: DOC website)

> Day 21
> 30.11.16
> Rakeahua Hut to Freds Camp Hut
> 12km

I HAD A DAMN good sleep because the fire was going all night and it was toasty warm. Dan had gone before I got up but he left me with a pile of goodies: some carrots, some zucchini, a little bit of fresh milk, a packet of tea bags, some egg noodles, a big chunk of blue cheese, some wet wipes, and — most importantly — that nice big deer heart. This was total luxury for me.

I was going to eat the heart for breakfast but I decided to save it for dinner. I planned to fry it up with half an onion and some garlic — I was going to make a feast.

I got up, made myself some freeze-dried butter chicken for breakfast and waited for Dad to call on the satellite phone about the kayak. After weeks of looking for a book in the huts, I finally found one that was worth reading — *Trog*, published by the University of Canterbury's tramping club. It was all these stories about epic journeys. It was really cool. There was a big section about things that had gone wrong — I quite enjoyed reading that! A cup of tea, some butter chicken and a good book: my life felt sorted.

That feeling didn't last long. Dad phoned and he hadn't been able to get hold of a kayak for me. I stood staring at the map of the island on the hut wall trying to work out what the hell I was going to do. I had to come up with another plan.

If only I'd flown over the island before I'd started.

That way I would have been able to see some of the cool places and I would have known where I wanted to go. I was completely lost. I had no idea what to do from here.

I got all worked up and worried about it. I called my mum and told her my problem. She talked to me about it and fortunately made me feel OK.

I decided I just had to get moving. I'd walk to the next hut along the track — Freds Camp Hut — and hopefully work out what to do once I got there.

I had dry boots for once. I was so excited about that. Unfortunately, it only took five minutes until I was knee-deep in mud. Oh, I hate the mud. I just had to walk through it — there was no way round it.

As I walked, I slowly formulated a plan. I was going to spend the next 10 days making my way back to Oban on and off the track, just having a bloody good time, doing things my way. It was about time for some goddamn fun. As I sloshed my way along the edge of South West Arm of Paterson Inlet towards Freds Camp Hut, a fantail flitted alongside me and my mood lifted a little bit.

That was until I hit the mud again. What looked like a shallow puddle turned out to be a knee-deep mud bog and I stepped into it, completely unsuspecting. It took a lot of energy to drag myself out of it. I just wasn't feeling at the top of my game, and slogging my way through the mud sure wasn't helping.

A bit of sunshine made a big difference. The bush was so nice to walk through — there were huge old trees and the undergrowth was beautiful green moss and ferns. It was so different to the scraggly greyness of the manuka scrub.

The bush was more open than what I had seen for a while. I saw a deer dart off into it at one point. It was also pretty damn flat all day, with only a few small ups and downs along the way.

I mostly watched my feet when I walked so I didn't trip up on anything, and I was doing just that when suddenly something darted out from under my feet. It was a kiwi! I just about stepped on it. They seem to like to sit there and do nothing until you're just about on top of them, then they shoot off really fast. It definitely didn't hang around! I watched it disappear into the lush green undergrowth.

My surroundings made me think: there's nowhere else in New Zealand that looks like Stewart Island. It's almost like *Jurassic Park*. You half expect a velociraptor to appear and take off with you, it's so untouched. The bush is so wild and lush, it's awesome.

Once I'd worked out what I was going to do for the next 10 days, my brain went back to its other favourite pursuit — dreaming about food. Ice cream, apple pie, cream donuts and pies were all still high on my wishlist!

I knew I needed to eat more but I couldn't because I didn't have enough food with me. I'd already eaten one of my spare meals at Rakeahua, so I had to start being a bit more careful again. Man, I was so hungry.

The day's walk was about 12 kilometres and it took me about six hours. I knew I was getting quite close to my destination because I could see the mouth of the South West Arm approaching. It was about 10 minutes before I arrived at the hut. The hut was at the bottom of a steep bit of track, and when I got down there it was awesome.

It was a really nice hut, with the most beautiful view of the sea. I watched the sea for a few minutes before going inside. There was a little beach with a jetty running out from it. Across South West Arm was the disused Silvertown mine, and I could also see up to Dynamite Point at the head of North Arm.

When I climbed the steps of the hut, I looked in the window. Oh my god! I could barely contain my excitement! I threw the door open, raced in and, sure enough, the most amazing thing was just sitting there on the table: a huge heap of food with a note that said just two, magic words: *Help yourself.* Thank you whoever you are!

There was custard powder, mashed potato flakes, even muffins. Muffins were up there on the list of things that I'd been craving so that was beyond awesome. I decided I was going to have some for breakfast with porridge, cinnamon and brown sugar.

I dumped my pack, got out of my muddy clothes, lit the fire and started to plan my menu for the evening. I was so happy. The one thing that made me even happier was that there was a knife in the kitchen drawer, so I could actually cut things up and I didn't have to resort to ripping them to bits with my teeth!

Outside, as if to reflect my mood, the sun was shining and a rainbow appeared over the bay.

That night I ate:

Starter: Four-cheese macaroni that someone had kindly left behind.

Main: Thinly sliced venison heart, seasoned with

paprika and fried in butter, with onion, garlic and zucchini, with a side of zucchini and blue cheese noodles. (Dan — you are freaking epic.)

Dessert: Cuuuuustaaaaaard. (Oh my god, I'd been dreaming of custard for so long. It was to die for. It was easily the best custard I'd ever eaten. I didn't know custard could be that good.)

It was the best goddamn meal I'd had in a very long time. It was all so good that I barely needed to wash the dishes, as I ate every last bit of every course. I ate so much I felt a bit sick but it was so worth it.

After dinner, I headed out to see if I could catch a fish off the wharf. For bait, I used one of the main arteries out of the deer heart. If I failed to get a fish, I knew I'd be OK as there were lots of mean-looking mussels out in the bay — plus I hadn't *quite* managed to eat everything in the hut.

Sitting at the end of the wharf with my line in the water, I was truly happy. Despite its not-great start, this had turned out to be one of the best days. This was the life!

Sitting at the end of the wharf with my line in the water, I was truly happy. Despite its not-great start, this had turned out to be one of the best days. This was the life!

> Day 22
> 1.12.16
> Freds Camp Hut (rest day)

I GOT UP AND made myself a caramel latte. Oh, yes! That was amazing. The sun was shining brightly, so I hung my solar panels on the washing line and went off to chop some wood using the hut's axe.

With the wood chopped, I cooked up some breakfast. I coated the leftover deer heart in potato flakes and Cajun spices, then I fried it up in a bit of coconut oil, so it went all crispy and delicious. I mixed it through a big bowl of noodles with blue cheese and cream. It was one wicked meal! It's kind of hard to understand if you've never been seriously hungry, but it was so good.

On the shoreline was a row of big ponga trees, green against the blue of the sky and the water. I sat out on the porch in the sun, put my feet up on the railings and started to read another book that I had found in the hut, about a guy who was the sole survivor of a shipwreck. The dumbarse who wrote it had decided to write it in pirate language! It was all 'arr' and 'yarrr' — it was the worst book I'd ever picked up in my life! When it wasn't pirate language, it was like posh nineteenth-century language. I couldn't understand half of it. I already struggle with normal writing, but pirate language with all these old-fashioned words that I had no idea what they meant . . . it was impossible. I got about 20 pages in and I gave up.

It was wonderful weather all day. I watched fish jump

and listened to kiwi call. After a couple of hours sitting in the sun, I started to think about food again, so I headed out to collect some mussels. There were heaps of them growing on the rocks just off the beach and they were really easy to get when the tide was low. I got enough to last me for a few meals. I cooked some up for lunch and they were delicious.

I spent a while in the afternoon sketching a picture of Ngaio from a photo I'd been carrying with me. I kept it protected with two layers of plastic the whole time so it didn't get wrecked. It was the single most important thing I had with me.

Then, when the tide came in a bit, I headed out to the end of the wharf to try my luck again at catching some fish. To increase my chances, I put a burley bag with a few smashed mussels into the water then baited my hook with another mussel. And boom! I got a fish. And then another fish. And then another one. That was dinner sorted.

I nearly dropped my camera in the water when I was fishing. It's waterproof and it wasn't that deep — I just really didn't want to go getting in there. There were lots of sharks in this particular bit of water. Big seven-gillers. I saw one just swimming around, minding its own business — but I'm sure if I was in the water with it, *I* would have been its business!

While I scaled and gutted the fish, I heated some oil on the stove. Then I fried up the spotties — the smell was out of this world. I made up some mashed potato from the flakes and served the fish on top of that. Yeah boy! That was one good dinner. Even though the fish were small they tasted delicious. I was very impressed with my catch.

I didn't do any cleaning. My gear was all still wet and dirty. I figured that I only had five hours to walk to Freshwater Hut the next day and there would be, you guessed it, fresh water! I was going to leave the ocean behind. Once I got to the next hut, I decided I would make a plan about doing some inland exploring.

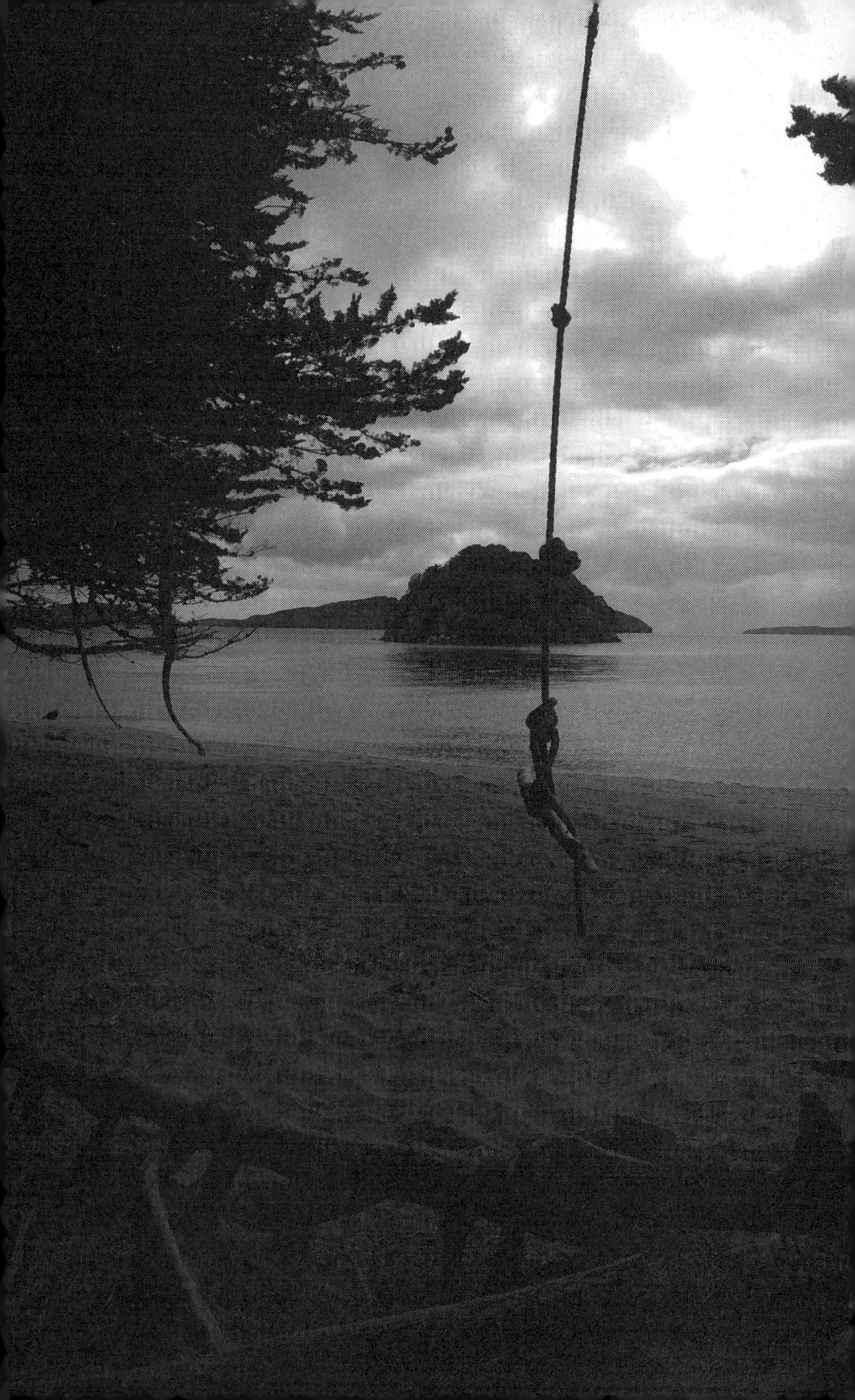

Chapter Nine
COMPANY

> Day 23
> 2.12.16
> Freds Camp Hut to Freshwater Hut
> 10 km

Having rested and relaxed, it was time to leave Freds Camp. I'd decided I'd stay on the Southern Circuit and head over to Freshwater Hut, which marks the end of the Southern Circuit and where the North West Circuit returns to Mason Bay to the west and to North Arm Hut to the east. It was about 10 kilometres away from Freds Camp and I reckoned it would take me about four hours.

ONCE I'D PACKED and had breakfast, I swept out the hut and made sure it was tidy. Then I pulled on my boots and walked out into the sun.

I was a bit sad to leave Freds Camp, as it had been so good to me! It was one of the most beautiful little bays I'd ever stayed at — so peaceful it was almost surreal. I stopped to take it in one last time before I climbed up the steps back to the main track.

It was amazing how much better I felt having rested and eaten well for a couple of days. The fact that the sun was shining probably helped things, too. It had dried a bit of the surface water on the track so I managed to stay dry for a little while. I was so stoked with the weather. It made such a difference to my whole experience.

The track started with steps going up into lush native bush. It was steep and muddy but not too muddy.

I stopped and listened to the kiwi call a few times, hoping I might see another one, but none showed themselves.

The bush along this part of the track was fantastic, too. It was lush and green, and most importantly it was easy to walk through. At some points the track was a couple of metres wide, and it was grassy and dry. There was a bit of mud but it was nowhere near as bad as it had been on the way into Freds Camp. All along the way, there were heaps of birds and they were all singing so loudly.

I dropped down out of the bush about two hours in and started walking through swamp. There wasn't much mud but there was so much water. I found myself trying to avoid it as best I could but unfortunately it was just about impossible to stay dry. I waded through the deep bits and jumped over the bits I could.

After a while I reached a dry section in the middle of the marshes. It was like a highway — every creature must have used this track. I followed it for about 3 kilometres until it ended and there was more swamp. I was pretty gutted about all the swamp, but I had to admit it was beautiful.

By about 2 p.m., I could see the next hut but I wasn't entirely sure how to get there as it was on the other side of a river. As I got a bit closer, I realised there was a really steep plank that led up a couple of metres to a swing bridge across the water. That swing bridge really gave me the shits. I almost wished I'd swum across the river instead!

There was nobody at the hut, so I took off my wet clothes and went for a big lie-down in the sun. The hut was about 3 kilometres from the river mouth, and the whole area was prone to flooding, which is why the swing bridge was so high above the river. It was hard to imagine what it must be like when the river was flooded.

Once I was unpacked, had done a bit of washing and put my solar panels on the roof to charge, I went back to lying outside in the grass. It was so good to feel the sun on my back. As I was lying there, I could hear something in the water. It sounded like someone swimming, which was strange, as there wasn't anyone else's gear in the hut. I went down to have a look and ran straight into a deer. It was right next to the hut — we were only a metre away from each other! It looked so scared when it saw me, it took off into the bushes, so I went back to relaxing in the sun.

Eventually I got hungry, so I boiled some water and had a freeze-dried butter chicken meal. While I was eating it a friendly fellow called Angelo came across the bridge. He was from America and we chatted for a while. It was nice to see another person again. Then a water taxi came to pick him up and I was alone once more.

I was stoked with how my day was going. The only thing that would have made it better would have been if I'd had company. I could have been playing cards with someone.

That thought gave me an idea. I decided to play cards

by myself. I made up a game where I was playing against a stick. I dealt two rows of four cards. The winner was whichever hand got a pair. In the very first hand, I got a pair, but then the stick got a pair. I couldn't believe that stick had got so smart with me. I had the last laugh, though — I hiffed that stick as far into the bush as I could. That'll teach it. All of which just went to show why I really needed someone else to play cards with.

I got a bit bored at the hut and decided to go for a little walk to see what I could find. Not only did I have no pack, I had no shoes and no shirt either. It was so good. While I was out wandering, I found a sign: 'This track is no longer maintained.' I had an idea, and headed back to the hut to make a plan. I was going to find out where that track went.

I was making a cup of tea when I heard voices approaching. I wasn't going to be alone after all! Four young guys my age appeared, carrying so much stuff. They were from Auckland and were on a boys' hunting trip, just having fun. They'd been on the island for two days and they'd had two days of sunshine. 'Wait until it starts raining!' I thought.

I told them about this little deer that had been hanging around. Not long after I'd finished, one of the guys yelled, 'Get the gun! Get the gun!' He grabbed the gun and ran off into the bush. He came back about five minutes later but he hadn't shot the deer. Then I was sitting looking out the window and saw it was right there. This guy just walked outside the hut, took aim, and *bang!* he shot the deer. It was 10 steps from the hut. Crazy. I couldn't believe they'd been that stupid to shoot it so close to the hut and the track. It was just really dangerous. They were young and excited so they just didn't think through the consequences of what could have happened.

That aside, one part of me was really sad because I was the one who had dobbed in the deer. The other part of me was so excited because it meant meat.

We chopped it up and the hunters took everything they wanted and left me the rest. I got in and boned out everything left over. I ended up with about 3 kilograms of fresh meat. I could have probably filled another bag if I'd wanted to. I took the liver, which I thought would be delicious. I decided I'd fry it for breakfast the next day.

I was charging some of my stuff with my BioLite when the guys offered me some of the venison they'd cooked with some spices — it was bloody beautiful. I made some mashed potato and had that for dinner. I was feeling fulfilled with life and my belly.

The meat I cut off the deer would keep me going for a couple of days at least. The good thing about it being cold at night was that I didn't have to worry about putting the meat in the fridge — I just hung the bag on a coat hook out on the porch and it stayed cold.

One of the guys let me borrow his knife for the rest of my trip because he knew I needed one. And not just any knife — a knife that his grandfather had left him. It had an antler handle and was made of hand-forged steel. He told me just to drop it back to him when I got back to Auckland (which I did). I was amazed that he would put so much trust in me.

I was so stoked to have lots of people around me.

I had definitely learned the value of being true to yourself and to the people around you. That was something I knew I really needed to change.

We chatted all night about lots of stuff. I was so much happier when I wasn't on my own.

✕

Hunting blocks

There are two different types of hunting blocks on the island — DOC ones and Rakiura Maori Land Trust ones. DOC have 35 different blocks, and the RMLT have nine. The blocks can all be booked online either through the DOC website (www.doc.govt.nz) or the RMLT website (www.visitrakiura.co.nz/hunting).

Most of the blocks have huts on them, but there are a few that just have campsites so they're cheaper to book. The huts are basic, each sleeping six people. You have to bring in all your own food, cooking stuff and bedding, as well as gas or coal to fuel the cooker and fire.

Because Stewart Island is such a beautiful place, DOC has some rules so that hunters don't affect the place negatively:

- ✕ Chainsaws, low-calibre rifles, shotguns and dogs are not permitted.
- ✕ Please leave huts and campsites clean and tidy, and take all rubbish off the island with you.
- ✕ Bury animal carcasses.

Target species are deer and possums. There are heaps of white-tail deer on the island so hunters usually end up with a good supply of venison. The other cool thing is that the blocks all touch the coastline, so there's also a chance to go fishing and diving — so long as you get better weather and water conditions than I did!

✕

Firearms Safety Code

If you are planning on going out hunting, make sure you're very familiar with the Firearms Safety Code, which can be found on the New Zealand Police website (www.police.govt.nz).

The seven firearms safety rules are:

✕ Treat every firearm as loaded.
✕ Always point firearms in a safe direction.
✕ Load a firearm only when ready to fire.
✕ Identify your target beyond all doubt.
✕ Check your firing zone.
✕ Store firearms and ammunition safely.
✕ Avoid alcohol or drugs when handling firearms.

✕

```
Day 24
3.12.16
Freshwater Hut (rest day)
4 km
```

I HAD A PRETTY good sleep, though I woke up a couple of times to hear people snoring, which was different as I was not used to having other people anywhere near me. It felt kind of great to be surrounded by people even while I was sleeping.

I woke up at 8 a.m., got up and went for a wee walk. I crossed the bridge and followed the river for a short time, then I sat there and enjoyed the morning bird call. It's one of my favourite things — just listening to nature. The noise the birds around the hut made in the morning was unreal. There were two tui in the tree right beside me. They were so close I could have reached out and touched them. It was a really still morning and there wasn't a ripple of wind on the river.

I had one more week to go on my adventure. I was going to be sad to leave this place. I really wanted to go home but it would be hard to leave. Stewart Island was the most beautiful place I had ever been.

So far in the journey I had learnt a lot about myself. The one thing I had learnt over everything else was that I don't like being alone. Being alone for me is pretty much the worst. A few days — that's awesome. A month? Nah. By being alone I mean being without friends. I had met so many people but to actually share these experiences with someone — the hard, the fun and the beautiful — would be so much more fulfilling.

I had had some bloody hard days over the last while, and as my trip was drawing to an end, I started to reflect on everything that had happened and to try to understand how it had changed me as a person. I had definitely learned the value of being true to yourself and to the people around you. That was something I knew I really needed to change. I needed to be comfortable with showing people the real me, and comfortable with doing what I wanted or needed to do, not what I thought other people wanted or needed.

Eventually I decided it was time for breakfast, so I went back to the hut and cut up my deer liver. I cooked it with some mashed potato. I couldn't get my head around the texture — kinda spongy. I ate as much as I could and started my day . . . well, I sat at the table for a good 45 minutes talking to the other people staying in the hut. Having people to talk to made me really want to come back here with my girlfriend, or with a bunch of mates — maybe get a hunting block like the guys from Auckland had done.

As well as the Auckland guys, a family had arrived at the hut the night before. They were from Belgium: a husband, a wife and a little girl who was five or six years old. That kid must have been so fit, as the family was hardcore. She was incredibly well behaved and had the cutest voice. Real cool.

The Auckland boys cooked up an eel and shared a bit with me, which was cool. I've eaten heaps of eel but they had cooked it with garlic and shallots for a little bit of extra flavour. It was pretty damn good.

Gradually, the hut emptied out and I decided to go on a little adventure. The cloud cover was thin and the wind was low so it was perfect exploring weather. I decided to head up either Rocky Mountain or the track I'd spotted the night before that had been closed since 2004. I had enough gear with me to stay overnight if I wanted to.

Eventually, Rocky Mountain won. I decided to climb up there and have a cup of tea. The start of the track, which was not far from the hut, was very mellow, then at the base of the mountain it pretty much climbed straight up. It wasn't too muddy. It was about 2.5 kilometres to the top, and at its highest point was 549 metres above sea level.

As I was walking I really started to notice the state of my feet. I could feel that they were covered in sores, because I hadn't been able to wash my socks properly in weeks. I was looking forward to being able to wash them soon. That and ice cream and a hot shower. Bliss. As I walked I tried to work out whether it was possible to eat ice cream and have a shower at the same time!

The track to the summit was sweet. While it was a bit of a climb, I made good time because I didn't have my pack on. Looking through the trees I could see the view was going to be amazing, so I climbed faster. About five minutes later the wind picked up and I felt a drop of rain, and then another. Then it started pissing down.

I was tempted to turn back but I carried on. Being wet and cold was so not fun and now the rain was wrecking my view. If only it would bloody stop!

Once I got beyond the bush line, the rain was joined by its old friend the wind, and sure enough, I couldn't see a thing. Actually, I could see one thing. I could see fog.

When I made it to the top, the weather was even worse. It was blowing and raining. But I decided I'd stop and have the cup of tea I'd promised myself despite the weather. I hid behind a rock and started my BioLite, which took ages. Then I realised there was only one thing missing for my cup of tea: water!

There were no streams up here so I had to sit and wait for the rain to fill my cup. I filled my cup up with rain dripping off this little plant — it was heinous. I put it on to boil and dropped in a tea bag. At least it wasn't going to take long to brew, as there was hardly any water. The cup definitely wasn't half full. Actually, it was about a quarter full. The funny thing was, it was raining too much to leave my little hiding spot and find more.

The cup of tea I made was so strong I could barely stomach it. At least it was hot, which I definitely wasn't. I was cold and wet. As much as I didn't want to leave my little shelter, it was time to head back down to the hut. There was a kiwi calling and I could see fresh footprints. No kiwi today, though.

As I walked, I shouted at the rain. I had a really good rant at the sky and then decided that if the weather was good the next day, I was going to head up the mountain again. I wanted to see that view!

The rain was so heavy that I was happy to get back down to the hut. It's hard to fully express the feeling of arriving at a hut in the rain and just knowing it's going

I was totally freaking out. There was blood all dripping off my hand, and the bleeding wouldn't stop.

to be warm — and if not warm, at least dry inside. That is an awesome feeling.

I got back down and it was only 2 p.m. Two o'clock and I had no idea what to do. While I was sitting there I noticed that someone had left a piece of wood they'd used as a walking stick outside. I cut the end off it and started whittling it with a little scalpel out of my survival kit. I didn't really start off making anything in particular but eventually I made a face. I decided I'd give it to Ngaio as a Christmas present.

There I was just whittling away and the next thing I know I pushed a little bit too hard, and the knife slipped down and went right into my hand. The blade was only about 3 centimetres long but the whole thing went into my hand. I pulled it out and there was fatty tissue sticking out and so much blood. I raced outside to avoid getting blood all over the hut.

Instantly, I went into panic mode. Not fix-my-hand mode, panic mode. I was walking around swearing my head off. 'What do I do? What do I do? This is so bad. Oh my god, what do I do?' I was totally freaking out. There was blood all dripping off my hand, and the bleeding wouldn't stop. (I still hadn't applied any pressure to the wound!)

I quickly grabbed my first aid kit and chucked some clotting agent into the wound. It probably needed stitches but I didn't have a suture kit. I managed to disinfect it and tape it up, but I knew I would have to be super careful over the next couple of days because if that thing opened up again, I didn't have the right first aid supplies to do it back up. Not good. I didn't have very many medical supplies left because of how many times I had cut myself on this journey.

Once I'd done the mending job, I was cold and I honestly didn't feel good. I really hoped that someone else would come to the hut that night. I was so annoyed with myself. My hand hurt so I had a couple of Panadol, which took the edge off.

Because of my hand, I changed my plans for the following day. I decided to stay at the hut and go on adventures from there for a couple of days.

Dinner was fantastic: venison from the day before, with some chilli paste on it. I could have eaten it ten times over. Then I did a little bit more whittling (away from my body this time, trying to miss my fingers).

Then I actually had a second dinner because I had so much food. I even used up my emergency packet of rice, which had written on it 'If you're eating this, then you're pretty much screwed. Good luck!' I still had lots of food left.

Apart from the injury, I was stoked with my day, and with my creation. It was the coolest thing I'd ever carved. When I'm out in nature and I've been there for a while, my creative side comes out. I love that. That's a big part of why I come out to these places. Just next time I won't do it on my own — or stick a knife in my hand.

Dealing with cuts

I had my fair share of cuts and scratches while I was on Stewart Island. Most of them were inflicted when I was whacking my way through the scrub, and they weren't too serious. Some of them got a bit infected, though.

The best thing to do with cuts is to make sure you keep them as clean and dry as possible. If it's quite a big cut, clean it with water that's been sterilised with an iodine tablet or, even better, keep some little tubes of saline in your first aid kit. Once it's clean, put some antiseptic cream on the cut and cover it with a dressing. Change the dressings every day if you can, to stop the cut from going septic.

For a more serious cut — like the one I got while I was carving — the main thing to remember is 'Don't panic!' I totally forgot that rule and ran around for a bit while I worked out what to do. I was more concerned with not getting blood in the hut than I was with fixing my hand. That's basically how not to do it. Your body has about five litres of blood in it and can lose half a litre before things get dangerous.

What you should do is:

- Elevate — raise the injured body part above the level of your heart. This means gravity will be on your side to help slow down the flow of blood.

✕ Add pressure — get a bandage or a piece of gauze out of your first aid kit and press it directly onto the wound. This will help slow down the bleeding and also give your blood more of a chance to clot, so don't be tempted to lift the bandage to check the cut. This will just tear out whatever clotting there is. If the bandage is soaked in blood, just chuck another one on top of it. This can take up to 15 minutes — just keep at it.

You might have seen people using tourniquets to stop bleeding — especially on TV. This should be used as a last resort only and only if you really know what you're doing, otherwise you could make things worse. Don't be tempted if you don't understand how to do it.

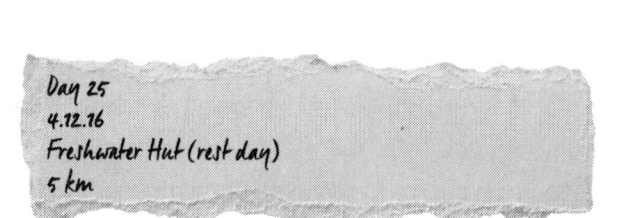

✕

> Day 25
> 4.12.16
> Freshwater Hut (rest day)
> 5 km

I SPENT THE DAY just having a long walk to nowhere in particular. The sun was shining so I figured I'd just get to somewhere I liked, sit down in the sun and do a bit more carving.

I had to take it a bit easier because of my hand. I needed to make sure it didn't get wet. If it got wet, then I would have to change the bandage, and I only had one more. Mostly, I hoped that someone else would show up at the hut with a full first aid kit so that I could get a new dressing on it. If they had sutures that would be even better, because every time I flexed my hand I could feel the cut wanting to open up.

Other than that everything was really good. I had no complaints whatsoever. I was so happy to be there on Stewart Island, even with the rain, even with the mud. I appreciated just how privileged I was to be there.

Before I set off for the day, I made Bolognaise for breakfast. There was still no one else in the hut so I made sure it was all clean and tidy, so it would be nice for anyone who arrived while I was out.

I got a bit distracted with my carving. It was going great — I'd got almost all of my Christmas presents made. I'd made the face for Ngaio and another one for Mum, then I'd carved a pineapple for my sister Brooke. The only thing I had left to create was a present for my dad, but I didn't know what to make him.

Eventually, at about 11.30 a.m., I headed off with a day bag with my tent attached. Over the bridge I went, then turned right down the track towards Mason Bay.

About 300 metres down the track on the right was the sign for the closed track. I just disappeared up it onto the Ruggedy Flats. It followed the Freshwater River, and up the valley it was so beautiful. There was just so much wildlife — so many birds and so many fish swimming around in the river.

The track hadn't been maintained for 12 years, so it was very overgrown and quite difficult to follow. I followed it for about an hour and a half then I set up my tent to shelter me from the sun and did some carving. I was in the perfect mood. I was just so at peace with everything — with what I was doing, with where I was. It was so beautiful. It wasn't raining, which made it ten times better. It did mean that the sandflies came out but they were beautiful, too. Holy smokes! There were like a thousand of them. Maybe not that beautiful . . .

It was so pleasant in the sun. I didn't even feel lazy because I had done a decent walk. I got my BioLite burning and boiled some water for my lunch, which was freeze-dried wild venison stew. Once I'd eaten, I sat and carved for a couple of hours — and I managed to cut myself again! This time it was my thumb, and though it wasn't as bad as the previous cut, it was still pretty bad. I wrapped it with my last big bandage.

After that, I packed up and had a quick drink from one of the tarns then walked back to the hut. I'd had my solar panels on the roof all day so I finally had full batteries to run my camera and my satellite phone. I didn't think that was going to happen!

When I got back to the hut there were two Australian guys there — Nick and Malcolm — who were walking the North West Circuit. They said they'd enjoyed it — except for the mud. (Nobody likes the mud.) I told them what I was up to and they talked about their travels and what they'd done. They shared some almonds and whisky with me, then I cooked up some venison with mixed herbs for dinner.

Over dinner, we mostly talked about travel and chose

a few walks we would do around the world. They had been to so many cool places — Africa, Russia, Europe — and had hiked in most of those places.

The guys went to bed early so I decided I was going to catch an eel. I went out, baited my hook with some venison and put my line in the water. I checked it about five times and there was nothing.

Just as the sun started to set, I headed back over the bridge to find an open space to watch it go down. I just stood there admiring the natural light as it slowly disappeared. It was so rewarding. On my way back to the hut, I decided to check my line one last time. It was jerking back and forth and I found a huge eel on it. I was so excited! I knew what breakfast would be.

I went to bed a happy chap. The day had been a great one. I didn't want to leave. The thought of walking out to Oban made me feel sad. But I tried not to think about it too much.

Day 26
5.12.16
Freshwater Hut
5 km (Rocky Mountain - again)

I WOKE UP TO the sound of the other men in the hut farting. It was pretty funny. They were great guys, though!

I did some cleaning then I cooked up my eel for breakfast. The skin went all crispy when I fried it up. I'm a huge fan of crispy-skinned eel. Love it! Because the water was so clean down here, the eels tasted really good. I shared it with Malcolm and Nick and they loved it, too.

Malcolm gave me a whole bulb of garlic. I was stoked about that, as it would add a bit of flair to my last few days of venison and eel. That food was fantastic and I knew I was going to miss it once I left the island.

Malcolm and Nick headed off for North Arm Hut at about 8 a.m. I went and sat out on the bridge over the river. The view from up there took in the river, Rocky Mountain and Mount Rakeahua.

A couple of days earlier I had headed up Rocky Mountain to get a good view and failed. Today, the skies were completely blue. There wasn't a cloud to be seen. It was easily the best day weather-wise that I'd had the whole time I'd been on the island, so I decided to head up Rocky Mountain again.

But first I wanted to do a bit more carving. I decided I'd make a ring for my dad. I decided on a ring because it was going to be the hardest thing for me to create. I made it out of a block of wood, and it took me freaking ages — like three hours. I really hoped he would like it. I put so much thought into it. Luckily, I didn't cut myself again.

With the ring done, it was time for lunch. I cooked up the last of the tasty eel, then packed up a small day bag to head up Rocky Mountain.

I had cut my foot the night before as I was jumping over a creek, and I was a bit worried about what it was going to look like after I put it in my boot with my manky socks. I knew it would probably get a little bit infected, but she'll be right, I thought — I only had a couple more days before I was going to walk out to Oban.

I put my socks on — they were dry! I didn't even wear my gaiters. I just wore shorts and a t-shirt.

The ground dried out so fast when there was no rain. It was almost like the island was one huge blocked drain slowly drying out — but way more awesome and less smelly than that.

I got up to the top of the hill in an hour. I stopped just before the bush line for a drink in a river, then carried on past where I had had my wet cup of tea the first time and continued higher towards the very top. It was marked with a huge cairn. I put a rock I'd picked up on top of the cairn then I climbed up onto it, letting out a mighty roar. I was so stoked to be there and the view was one of the most spectacular I have ever seen. I could see all the way from the Ruggedy Mountains to the Deceit Peaks, where I had camped out on my first night off-track. There was the Freshwater River snaking its way down the flats. It looked like a dragon. I had never seen anything quite as amazing as this place.

I turned on my phone to take some photos and the cell signal was strong so I decided to go live on Facebook and Instagram to show everyone the stunning view that I was looking at. It honestly was the most incredible view on the island.

After that I called Ngaio and we chatted about all the cool things I had been doing and how nice it had been to escape from social media for 30 days, which was kind of funny given I'd just done a live feed from up here!

After an hour of exploring the tops, I headed back to the hut. Halfway down the hill I slipped over and landed on my hand. My cut opened back up and I was in pain. But it didn't matter. Nothing was going to take away the good feeling that this place had given me.

Dinner was the last of my meat. I was stoked when I cooked it and realised that after three days it had aged, which improved its flavour and texture. I was in food heaven, eating like a king for one more night. It would be freeze-dried food, damper and dripping from now on until Oban. I had the last of my rice with that, then had a second dinner to make my pack lighter (oh, all right, and just because I felt like it).

I boiled some water, cleaned my dishes and sat down to talk to the woman and her daughter who were staying the night after having walked over from Mason Bay. My hut mate had some colouring pencils so I asked if I could borrow a few to make one of my carvings more colourful. With a bit of colour on it, the pineapple I'd carved for my sister looked more like it was meant to. Brooke was going to love it.

I decided to head to Mason Bay the next day to get the food that I had left at the hunters' hut — if it was still there. The forecast wasn't great but I crossed my fingers for rain and not hail. I figured I'd stay at Mason Bay for two nights, so I could go down to the southern end of the beach and explore, then I'd head back to Freshwater Hut before my final two days back into Oban.

Sitting in the last of the day's sun, I realised that this next stage of my trip would be very important. I knew that when I got back after this journey, I wouldn't have time to reflect on what had happened and I wouldn't have time to relax. I'd been going hard for 26 days, so I decided to use my last few days to really reflect on what I had done and what I wanted to do next.

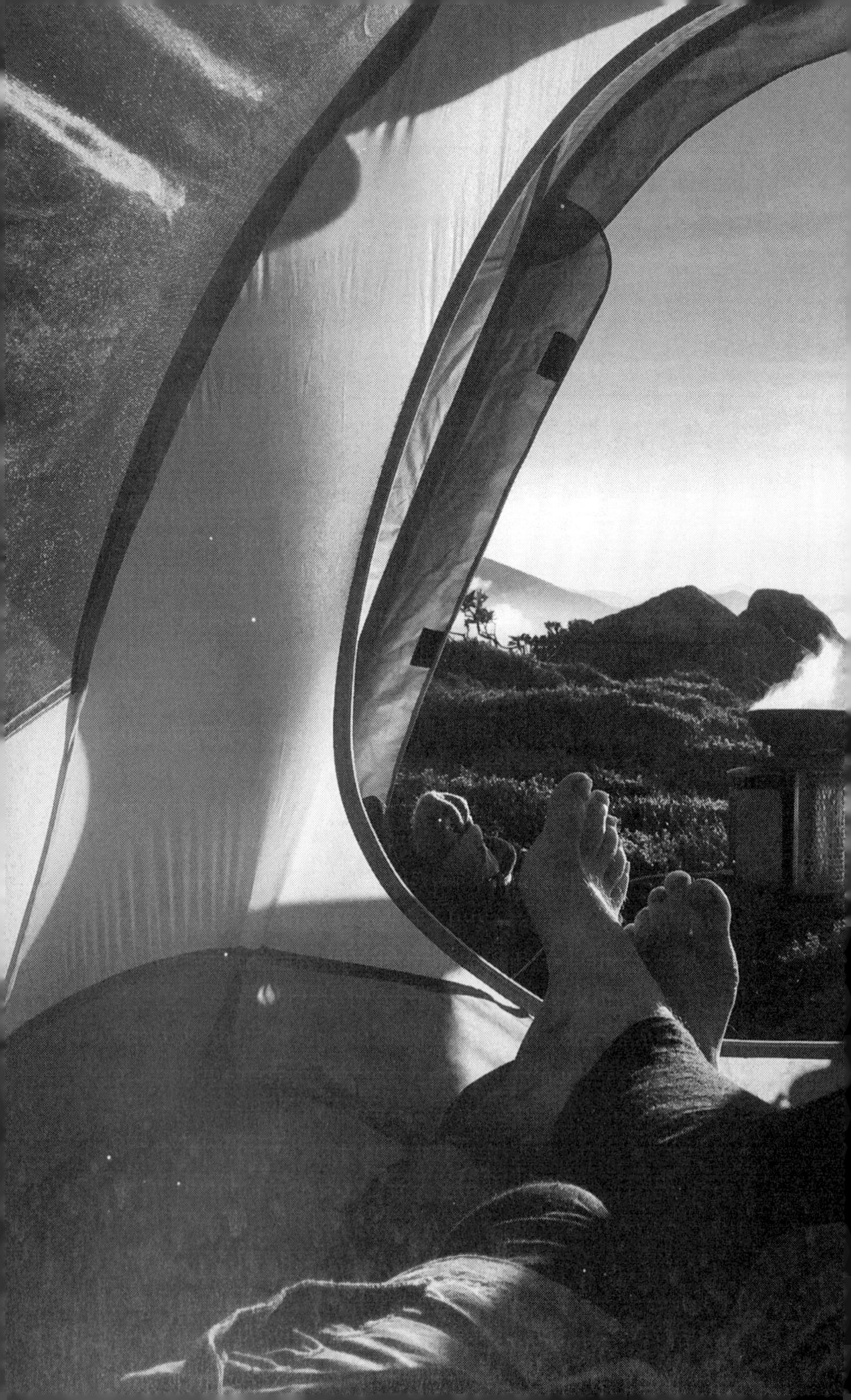

Chapter Ten
REFLECTION

> Day 27
> 6.12.16
> Freshwater Hut to Mason Bay Hut
> 15.5 km

I had an awesome sleep and dreamt about making pancakes: a hot stack with maple syrup and fresh banana with a side of bacon.

I STARTED MY DAY extra early, to get to Mason Bay in plenty of time. Leaving Freshwater Hut, the track was wide and flat. I was walking through the low-lying swampland that I had seen from the top of Rocky Mountain.

It was so cool to see the history along the way — the old bridges, the drains the early settlers had dug to drain the swamp and the odd bit of metal rusting away. I was walking on an old road that had been built in the 1920s so that people could use horses to drag things from Freshwater Hut, where they could get to by boat, to Mason Bay where they used to farm. It was hard to imagine them farming anything, as not a lot grows here other than scrub. There was lots and lots of scrub and I was pretty sure sheep didn't eat that. From my experience, nothing eats scrub, things just get stuck in it.

As I was walking, a plane flew overhead. It was so weird to hear that noise after so many weeks of just being in the quiet of nature. I figured it must have been heading towards Mason Bay.

For most of the time, the track followed a river until it turned into boardwalk and I found myself walking on top of a boggy swamp. It was so nice to not be in them for once. I took my time checking out all the sights. At Island Hill, there was an old homestead and woodshed. It was a pity it wasn't open because I could see a lot of old books inside the homestead, and I still wanted a good book to read.

At the homestead I met a hunter and his wife and chatted to them for a bit. I told them I was going down to the hut to fetch the food I had left there. They reckoned there was only rice left. I was a bit gutted and hoped that they were wrong.

About halfway down the track, I reached a point where the sun was shimmering through the trees — it looked so beautiful. I was looking up and as my eyes fell back on the track there was a deer no more than 3 metres in front of me. It was standing at the end of a long, straight bit of track and was completely framed by manuka scrub. I froze so that it wouldn't run off, and it froze, too. It just stared at me for a while. I felt so in touch with nature. It slowly turned around and bounded off down the track. I followed the deer a fair way before it realised I was there and then it took off into the manuka scrub.

The hunters' hut was a bit over a kilometre past Mason Bay Hut, so I decided to drop my pack at the main hut then head down to Martins Creek and find out what was still there. I was so excited at the thought of collecting the food I had left behind when I was first there that

It was so cool to see the history along the way — the old bridges, the drains the early settlers had dug to drain the swamp and the odd bit of metal rusting away.

I ran down the beach. It took me about 15 minutes.

When I arrived I found only the flour and dripping was left from the food that I had left behind. The hunters had got it wrong about there only being rice left — that was the only thing that had gone.

And then I did something bad. In the hut was a bag of really, really tasty-looking home-made biscuits. I couldn't help myself and I ate one. They weren't mine. I felt so bad about it, as I knew I'd stolen food off someone. I felt really bad . . . but they were so tasty.

I walked back down the beach with my goods. I was so happy with the flour and dripping. I was going to have pancakes, and they were going to be amazing. As I walked, I got dive-bombed by some crazy seagulls and then came across a sea lion that was fast asleep. Well, it was until I came along. It came rushing towards me and growled. I roared at it to let it know I wasn't scared — but I was really. It's quite amazing how fast they can move across the sand.

Coming back to Mason Bay Hut, a lot of memories returned. It was good to be there a second time — different faces, different stories. There were two nice ladies from Christchurch in the hut who gave me some capsicum, an apple and a plaster for my hand. About 20 minutes later three more people showed up at the hut. They had been walking the Southern Circuit. I told them my stories and they shared their 16-year-old whisky with me. I'm not much of a drinker, but it was good. They also shared their dessert with me: ginger crunch with a vanilla pudding. It was so delicious.

I made myself some of the best damper ever. It was also probably the most unhealthy thing you could eat anywhere — damper cooked in boiling-hot dripping then covered in peanut butter. So good!

I caught an eel for breakfast the next day and left it marinating in garlic, herbs and oil. I had had a great day and I couldn't wait to walk to the Gutter, which is a narrow channel between the bay and the Ernest Islands, at the southern end of the beach the next day. The trip would take about six hours all up so I decided I would have lunch there and then walk back.

I went to sleep feeling excited about the coming days. My headspace was totally different to anything I'd ever experienced. I felt great about everything I had done and everything that was still to come.

Now that the trip was nearly over, I was both nervous and excited about getting back to the real world. Here there had been no real responsibility other than feeding myself. Even though that had been difficult at times, it was still an amazing way to live.

Hut etiquette

I'm quite bad at hut etiquette. The ideal hut companion for me would be someone who didn't care that I had my stuff everywhere. When I come into a hut, I walk in, open my bag, take all my stuff out and start drying it. It's always wet. I don't have food, so I'll drag in a dead eel or a rat. I'll be preparing a rat on the table in front of people. They'll be like 'What are you doing?! Do you want some food?' and I'll be like 'I'm OK, I'll just eat this.'

If I haven't spoken to anyone in days, I'll want to ask heaps of questions: 'What do you do? You're a doctor? Do you see some gnarly stuff? I hurt my foot — can you help me with this?'

I would do my best to work out if people didn't want to talk to me and I'd leave them alone. I always tried to remember that a lot of them had come from their super-busy, loud lives for some peace and quiet.

When you're using a hut, you're responsible for leaving it as tidy — if not tidier — than you found it. There's no room service out in the bush! Here's DOC's Hut Users' Code:

- Keep huts clean and tidy. A broom, brush and pan are provided — please use them, and leave muddy boots outside.
- Conserve gas when using gas heaters and cookers. During cooking always open a window or door to allow dangerous carbon monoxide fumes to escape. Keep an eye on boiling water/food, and be sure to turn gas heaters off overnight and when you leave.
- Take care using wood burners, keep the fire contained and never leave it unattended. Only burn dead, dry wood and be careful with hot ashes. Make sure the fire is extinguished before leaving. Use wood sparingly

and replace any you use for the next visitors.
- ✕ Share huts with others by being considerate, make room for late-comers and keep quiet if others are sleeping. Share boiled water with other trampers to help conserve gas.
- ✕ Carry it in, carry it out — recycle *all* your rubbish. Take two bags, one for recycling and the other for rubbish/food scraps to carry out with you and dispose of responsibly.
- ✕ No smoking in huts. Take your cigarette butts out with the rest of your rubbish.
- ✕ Hunters must follow the Firearms and Safety Code.
- ✕ No dogs allowed inside huts.
- ✕ Before leaving, close doors and windows securely.
- ✕ Always pay hut fees.

(Source: DOC website)

✕

Day 28
7.12.16
Mason Bay Hut to the Gutter (return)
16 km

I WOKE UP AT 8.30 a.m. and got up to make a cup of coffee. I made that coffee last so long. For breakfast I had pancakes, shallow-fried in fat with peanut butter on them. I followed that up with an eel fried in dripping.

I got a stick and tied a bit of plaited flax to it, then I tied the eel to the flax. It looked like a little fishing rod, but it was designed to make it easier for me to turn the eel in the pan. Such a good invention!

The lovely ladies from Christchurch wanted to taste it, so I cooked them a fillet. They were very happy. It was a great atmosphere in the hut, with lots of things going on. One of the ladies gave me the world's nicest ginger caramel and an apple.

With plenty of food in me, I set off for the Gutter, about two hours away. It was overcast when I left just after 9. It started raining about 30 minutes later and it didn't stop for the length of the beach.

The walk was pretty straightforward. It was flat the whole way — making for quite sore feet by the end of it.

I did a lot of thinking as I made my way down the beach. It was so nice to be able to use that time to reflect on my wild adventure. It had been hard and wet and cold. But it had been so good for me and now, looking back, it had been really beautiful and quite incredible.

I walked along the high-tide mark, looking for treasure to pick up. I found a few really cool things like a whale's eardrum and also a cool rock. I had no idea what I was going to do with them but I was sure I'd think of something.

As I walked along, a plane flew quite low overhead — this one was definitely heading for Mason Bay, as it looked as if it was coming in to land at the other end of the beach. It came in low and fast and looked like so much fun.

The next thing I knew, it was taxiing back past me using the beach as a runway. Ahead in the distance I could see a group of four people standing watching it fly out. They had just been dropped off. What a way to travel!

I walked up to them and said, 'Don't you feel like you've been dropped off in the middle of nowhere?'

They laughed and agreed. There were two ladies from Wanaka and a young couple from the Hawke's Bay. They were headed to Mason Bay Hut but decided to get dropped at the southern end of the beach to get a look at the Gutter.

One of the ladies said to me, 'We thought you might have been Wildboy . . .'

'I am indeed!' I replied.

They looked quite surprised, and laughed. 'We were just talking about you! We saw you on telly. We thought it might have been you but the pilot said it couldn't be because you were away round the other side of the island.'

I quickly explained what had happened and told them I'd come back to Mason Bay because it was so beautiful and I wanted to explore it some more. It was hard for me to believe that they had seen me on TV standing on this very same beach 16 days earlier. One of the first questions they asked me was what I'd had for breakfast that morning. I was happy to tell them I'd had eel! We decided we'd all go off exploring together, and I was so happy to have company.

It was low tide and it was fantastic. I'm so glad I walked down there to see it. The surf was huge. It was crashing onto the rocks and exploding into the air, but if you turned around and looked into the bay, it was still and flat like a millpond.

There was only a small bit of water between the mainland and the inner islet of the Ernest Islands. I would have loved to have gone across but the water was just way too cold to get into, and given how narrow the passage was it was probably dangerous as well.

I invited them to join me when I walked up to the Kilbride homestead, near the Gutter. A sheep farm had been established at Kilbride in 1902. The last sheep were only removed from there in 1995, which was pretty hard to imagine.

We walked up to the homestead cross-country, instead of following the track. I found a deer head and guts that looked fresh — I'm sure it would have only been a few days old. I also found a life ring that I hung up in the hut. I think that this spot was one of the coolest places I visited on the island.

The young couple shared their lunch with me — pita bread with coleslaw and dressing. The two ladies shared some chocolate with me. Oh god, that was so good. They also gave me a pear. These people were so generous. They were just filling me up with all these delicious treats.

I made my way back with the young couple, as they walked at the same speed as me. It was the second time I'd walked with someone and it was nearly in the same place. We talked about all the places they'd been and it was so inspiring. It made me want to travel the world, which was something that I knew Ngaio would be excited to do with me.

When I got back to the hut, who should be sitting there but Ant from day two! He had 30 days' worth of food and was off on another awesome adventure. Man, it was great to see him. He was a really cool character. I found his lifestyle inspiring.

I cooked up some more pancakes with my dripping and flour, and when I went inside Ant offered me a packet of macaroni cheese. Oh my goodness, it was good. I was sitting outside eating that when the ladies I'd met earlier in the day came out and gave me some quinoa with sun-dried tomatoes. It had been a real day of food. I didn't ask for any of it, people were just so generous.

Once I'd eaten and had some good chats with everyone, I climbed up on a sand dune to watch the sun set. The view across the sand dunes towards the setting sun was amazing. The sky started out blue and with pale fluffy clouds, which turned a mixture of pale pink and soft yellow.

When the sun really started to drop, I just sat and stared at it. I stared for about five minutes and it didn't even hurt my eyes. It was just a big ball of pure energy slowly slipping into the ocean. It felt almost like it was being extinguished by the sea.

After the sun had gone, I went on a kiwi hunt down on the beach with my old mate Ant. I think he has it sorted. I'd love to go on a trip with him one day soon.

I lay awake late that night. It had been awesome meeting all these people, talking to them and connecting with them. It was lovely to have company. The difference between the people I met on the island and the people I met on my past travels is that these people were all trekkers — they were on the trail. They had trail stories and they loved travelling. It was quite different from my trip around New Zealand where I mostly met people in their own homes.

This was going to be a hard trip to finish. I wasn't excited to leave this place anymore. Having spent so much time out on the tracks and in the wild just made me want more people to get back into nature and appreciate nature for what it is. There are too many people who have forgotten what nature is, or who have never been shown it. Nature is the greatest energy source in the world.

I came to Stewart Island to go on a mission, but I ended up learning about myself, recharging my nature batteries and plugging into my own life. Without that connection, I was lost. It is worth more than anything to me.

Without escapes like this, life becomes cluttered, it becomes a drag, it becomes a big confusion of stuff, places and people. It's important to sit back, reflect, relax and enjoy nature's gifts.

> Day 29
> 8.12.16
> Mason Bay Hut to Rocky Mountain
> 16.5 km

I GOT UP REALLY early and was out kiwi hunting before 6 a.m. The sun was just coming up and it was still super cold, but the sky was clear and the air was still. I hadn't had a very good night's sleep — partly because someone in the hut was snoring and partly because I had overloaded on food. I just wasn't used to eating that much.

I spent the early part of the day just out walking and really looking at what was around me — seeing the sun shine through a newly spun spider web or the dew forming droplets on the tussock. I climbed up a hill behind the hut and watched as the sun rose higher. There was a light layer of mist along the valley, and as the sun slowly burned it off, the surrounding hills revealed themselves. In the distance I could hear kiwi calling. It was so peaceful just sitting there watching the day start. I love watching morning begin. It makes me wonder if other creatures also enjoy this part of the day.

I walked down to the hut for breakfast, then packed my gear and headed back towards Freshwater Hut. Unfortunately, Ant had already gone, and I was sad to have missed the chance to say goodbye to him.

On my way back to Freshwater, I decided to explore the old farm at Island Hill a bit more. Outside one of the sheds there was a rusty old tractor. It looked quite weird, as the body of it was really stuffed but the tyres looked almost like new. To entertain myself, I jumped on it and

Without escapes like this, life becomes cluttered, it becomes a drag, it becomes a big confusion of stuff, places and people. It's important to sit back, reflect, relax and enjoy nature's gifts.

pretended to be a farmer, complete with floppy hat and a piece of grass to chew on. I wasn't just any old farmer though — I farmed kiwi!

'I saw two kiwis this morning and tried herding them in with my tractor. They didn't like the tractor much. Maybe I should cover the tractor in feathers so they think it's a kiwi. Maybe I should put a little note on the back of it saying "Free rides" — maybe they'd jump on in and get a ride down to the woolshed here. Just so you know, it's not actually a woolshed. It's actually a feather shed. It's been here since 1930, when the feather trade was really booming.' You get the general idea . . . I think it was probably a sign of just how much I'd missed having people to talk to.

As I walked along, I was so happy I started singing. It didn't take long until someone heard me. I came around the corner and the Wanaka ladies and a doctor were watching a kiwi — until my singing scared it away. I walked with them for a little while and we shared our stories with each other.

Around midday, I was walking with the doctor when she stopped suddenly and pointed into the manuka. It took me a moment to see what she was pointing at — it was a Stewart Island robin. These birds are so cute. They're about the size of a sparrow and grey or brown with a white patch on their fronts. The little bird hopped around in the trees, then — as I stood completely still — it dropped down onto the ground and closely investigated my feet for a couple of minutes before flying away, chirping happily. Before too long, he came back with his mate and they flitted around in front of me.

I found out later that they like following people — or other birds — and feeding on insects in the dirt disturbed by our feet. It's amazing how fearless they are as they hunt for food. They nest on or near the ground, which means that they are easy targets for rats and other predators. Their numbers dropped as low as 500 at one point, but there's been heaps of work done since to protect them and, while they're still at risk, they're no longer endangered.

Hanging out with the robins, I was just happy not to be under pressure and on a tight timetable. It was so good just to be able to hang out and watch them for as long as I wanted. This was the life.

Eventually, I tore myself away from the birds and headed back to Freshwater Hut. I got there early in the afternoon. As it was such a hot day, I decided there was only one thing for it — I was going to go for a swim.

There was a jetty on the river for boats to moor at that had a ladder down into the water. I climbed down into the river with all my clothes on. If I was going to get wet, I might as well do a bit of washing as well!

Once I got out and got dry, I relaxed in the sun for a few hours then I headed back to the hut and hung out with my new friends for a while. Then I decided to go on another little adventure. Rocky Mountain was calling my name again!

The weather was so nice that I decided to take my pack and spend the night up there. It was going to be cold but I couldn't wait to see the night sky from the top and then watch the sunrise in the morning. I couldn't think of a better way to spend one of my last nights on the island.

Even though I was going a bit slower than the previous time because I had an extra 25 kilos on my back, I was happy as I walked along the track. It was a hard slog up that steep hill, though. My legs were burning. In fact, it got so hot that I had to take off my pack and strip off my shirt. Who would have thought that after all the terrible weather I'd been through I'd be walking topless!

Because it was so hot and I had all that extra weight on me, I took plenty of opportunities to stop and drink from the streams by the track. The water was cool and delicious. I filled up my water pouches as well. This time I'd definitely have enough for a cup of tea at the top if I wanted one.

I felt like I could see the whole island opening out in front of me. I put up my tent just as the sun was starting to get lower in the sky. I made sure that the opening faced right out to the west so I could see the sunset from inside. The wind was pretty chilly so I put a few more layers of clothes on and waited.

The sunset was totally worth the wait. It was surreal, even better than the one the previous night. These moments, these are what adventures should be about.

I had enjoyed the day so much I didn't want it to end. It was so cool being out there just living, being myself. That night I sat watching the stars. I counted three shooting stars before falling asleep.

Island Hill Run

The place where I mucked about on the tractor is called Island Hill Homestead. It was the heart of the Island Hill Run, which was the island's longest-running sheep farm.

It was first settled in 1884 by a man called William Walker. He built a little house there that was added on to and is now in the middle of the homestead building.

In 1902, the Kilbride Run was established — where I walked to with the people I'd met off the plane. That was run by William Thompson, whose family had managed Island Hill since taking it over in 1898.

A few more families farmed Island Hill until Tim and Ngaire Te Aka took over in 1966. They were the last people to farm sheep on the property, and they left in 1985. As well as farming sheep, Tim and Ngaire also did some live-deer recovery to subsidise their income, which wouldn't have been much given that they would have had to ship everything they needed over from the mainland, then get it brought up the Freshwater River before they picked it up and lugged it across the track.

The homestead is now owned by DOC and they use it for their staff to stay in, but they're happy for people to have a walk around and check out the buildings. If you're lucky they might even invite you in for a look!

> Day 30
> 9.12.16
> Rocky Mountain to North Arm Hut
> 12 km

AT ABOUT 2 A.M., I rolled out of my tent so I could watch the stars. I saw five or six shooting stars and lots of satellites peel over. The skies down here are so clear.

I went back to sleep and woke again three hours later to watch the sunrise. As awesome as the sunset had been the night before, the sunrise was pretty incredible, too. It looked like fire over the horizon, and as the sun slowly climbed, everything began to warm up — including the wind. I sat there with a cup of coffee and some muesli and just really enjoyed that moment up there on the mountain.

It was going to be another beautiful day — the second to last of my adventure. I couldn't believe that I'd been out here for 30 days of crazy, epic, awesome, relaxing, insane adventures. It had been a wild ride. And tomorrow, it would all be over.

I tried not to think about that too much because it made me sad. I had always known that I was going to hit this moment when I realised that this was so amazing that I didn't want to leave.

Apart from being sad about this adventure being over, I was happy — happier than I'd been in a long time. The dramatic change that I made in deciding to do this journey for me, rather than for the goal of walking around the coast, had really affected me. The journey changed *because I wanted it to*. It changed because I wasn't having fun. By changing it I taught myself some pretty important lessons. Do what makes you happy. I preach that all the time but I hadn't been practising it. From that point on, I decided I was going to do what makes me happy. If that makes other people happy, that's even better.

I packed up my tent and all my gear then was already heading back down the track by 7 a.m. I really enjoyed the walk down and made sure I took time off to stop, sit in the sun and admire the views.

It was a good thing I got away early, because I realised as I walked that I'd left my rain jacket in Mason Bay. The forecast was for it to rain heavily the next day so I was going to need that jacket if I didn't want to get absolutely soaked. I thought for a while about whether to go back and get it, but decided that as tomorrow was the last day, it didn't really matter if I got wet! Then I had a thought — maybe I'd left it at Freshwater Hut when I'd stopped off on the way up Rocky Mountain. I decided to stop in and check, as it was only a short detour from my planned route through to North Arm Hut.

It turned out I hadn't forgotten it at all. I found it tucked into my pack liner when I stopped at the bottom of the Rocky Mountain track. Whew! I called into the hut anyway and said goodbye to the friends I'd made there before heading to North Arm.

About five minutes after I left, a kiwi ran out in front of me. It raced off into the bushes. Just moments later another kiwi came into view. I was so shocked. Two in one day! I felt so lucky. I didn't expect to see any because two determined Germans had charged off ahead of me and I thought they would have scared off any birds as they went.

After that I got into walk mode and really started motoring. The track from Freshwater to North Arm Hut was about 11 kilometres and it was quite a tricky walk. There were a lot of steep bits, which were covered in roots, and there were some slippery, muddy bits, too. Even though I had to focus on where I was walking, I still had time to reflect on what I'd learned over the past month.

Most people have become so disconnected from reality. We're incredibly connected in so many other ways, with phones, TV, radio, social media . . . but we're really disconnected from life. And then there's virtual reality. Who the hell wants virtual reality when you can have real reality! I just feel like we need to take a step back. Technology has its place but nature can't be forgotten. Ten minutes a day in nature can change everything.

When I say nature, it doesn't have to be trudging through the bush. It can be going to the park, hanging out in the garden, lying on the grass — just connecting with everything that's around you naturally. Nature is life. Technology should always come second to life. Nature is a great place to learn, to really understand who you are.

My deep thoughts were soon interrupted by a couple of obstacles thrown in my path — quite literally. A couple of big trees had fallen over the track. There was a tiny space between them and I had to work out how to wriggle my way between them. Somehow, I managed to lie on my back and squish my pack down enough to just make it through. Yes, I could have taken off my pack but this way was way more fun!

Nature is life. Technology should always come second to life. Nature is a great place to learn, to really understand who you are.

Speaking of fun, I came across a big waterfall along the way so I stripped off and had a shower. It was a hot day and the water was so refreshing. I felt alive. I lasted a few seconds in the cold water before I ran out into the sun to dry off.

After lunch, I decided I would try my luck walking along the coast to the hut. The tide was very low so it was easy. I was walking through the water for most of the afternoon, which was a welcome change. I found some nice fat mussels in the deeper water, and filled a bag for dinner. You know you're somewhere really plentiful when you're picking and choosing the mussels you want!

Up ahead, the hut came into view. I walked across the muddy bay towards some wooden steps, and when I climbed back off the coast, it didn't take a genius to work out where the North West Circuit ended and the Great Walk began. The Rakiura Track was like a gravel road!

The North Arm Hut was quite different to all the other ones I'd stayed at. There were 24 bunks and the place was huge. There were quite a few sleeping bags already on beds so I knew that it was going to be a busy night.

Once I'd dumped my pack, I went back down to the water. It was fairly shallow for quite a long way, so I waded right out and had another swim. The water here was so much warmer than it had been elsewhere on the island, but I reckon the sun being out might have had something to do with that.

Back at the hut, I sat outside and cooked up some mussel fritters on my little stove for my dinner. Inside was busy with people cooking, chatting, sorting their gear and doing their dishes. It was weird to be around so many people after so long on my own. It made me wonder how I'd cope with being back in Oban the next day. I sat at the table and quietly wrote the last entry in my diary as the busyness went on around me.

The diary entry ended like this:

By this time, people had showed up at the hut. Lots of people. Like 17 people. They were all in Great Walk mode. I love the people you meet off trail and in back-country huts. They are like-minded. Here they are very touristy but that's OK. I met a cool German guy called Max. He joined me for a swim. It was cool to hang out with someone my own age. I decided to share the mussels with him. He didn't have a cooker so I cooked them up for him.

The birdlife here is amazing. There's so many kaka screaming around everywhere. The tui are so loud. I needed more food so butter chicken and pasta it was. I was treated to a Tim Tam from Max. He made my day with that . . . I only hope it doesn't make me sick! Tomorrow I will walk back out to Oban by four. I'm looking forward to relaxing once I'm done but not too much. I don't want to get out of my fitness regimen. I need to see my love. I'm so sad this is all over but I'm so excited.

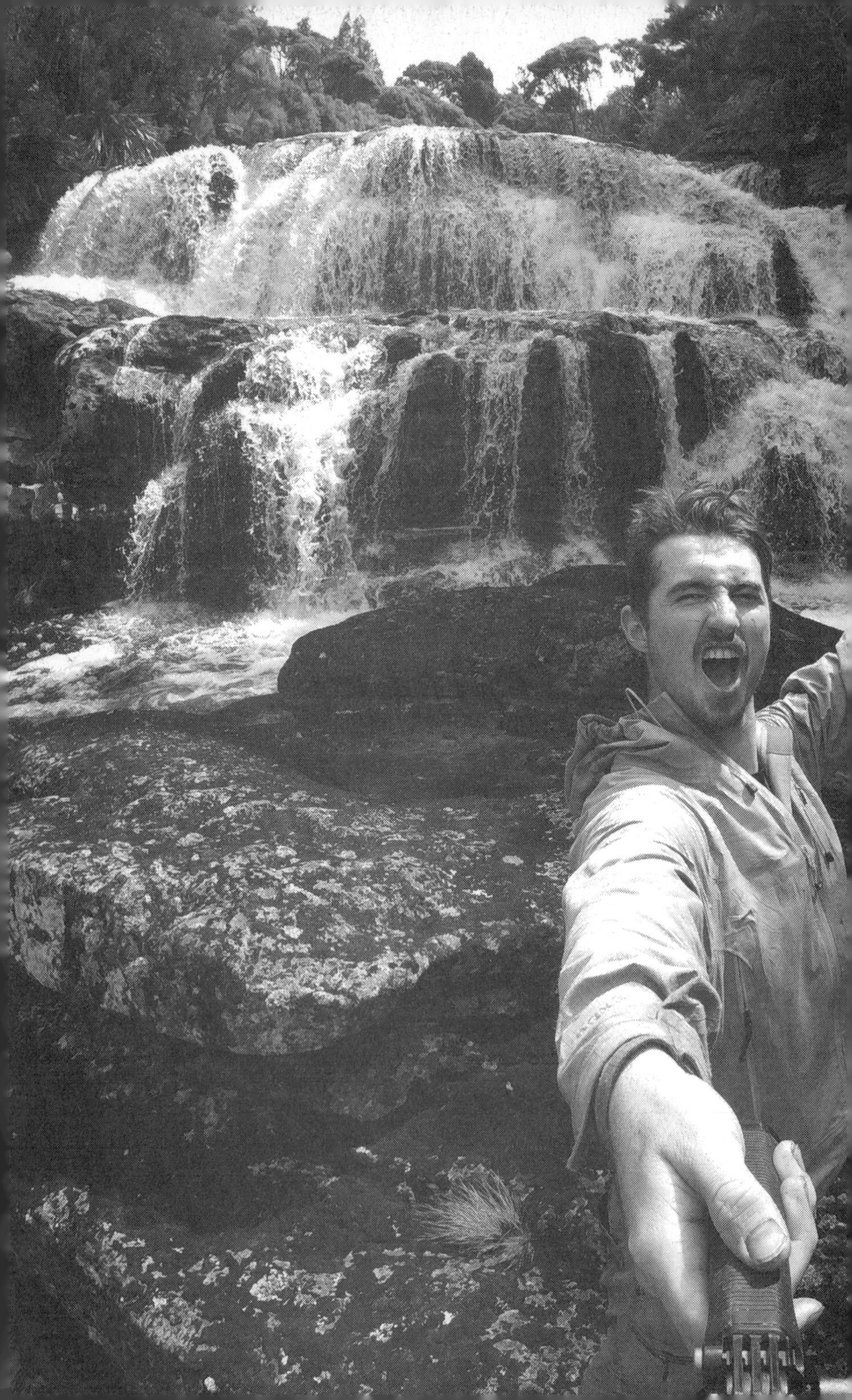

Chapter Eleven
THE FINISH LINE

> Day 31
> 10.12.16
> North Arm Hut to Oban
> 12 km

Walking-out day. Pizza and chips and beer, here I come!

I WAS WOKEN UP by another snorer. It was so strange sharing a hut with 16 strangers.

My last video diary recorded exactly how I was feeling:

It's the morning of day 31. This is the final walk. I'm in North Arm Hut. It's really windy and rain is forecast. This was my last night in a hut.

The feelings I have are really hard to describe. I really want to go home but then at the same time I really don't. On the good days I have so much fun, but on the bad days being on my own is really miserable.

I'm confused. I'm torn between two worlds. But this trip has been amazing. It's been a real eye-opener to different lifestyles. I know this won't be the last trip I go on but it might well be the last solo trip.

I love finding an amazing campsite, a beautiful view or a big waterfall. This lifestyle is hard in so many ways but it's amazing. Without this lifestyle I would be lost. I believe that the connection that I have with the outdoors is incredibly strong. It's the best drug in the world. It makes me high on life when I'm out here. I crash every now and then but for the most part everything I look at is beautiful.

I feel like I can really be myself out here. I can do weird stuff, I can just be a human. I don't have to pretend in order to fit in to some society or group. I can just be me. You need to do what you love even if that means changing your plans.

Walking around the coast of Stewart Island is totally possible. It could have been done. But I didn't see the point — I wasn't having fun. All I could see was scrub so I decided to have some fun. Over the past seven days I've had so much fun. I've met some cool people, been to beautiful places and seen nature at its best. It's been nice escaping from the hardship.

THE WEATHER FORECAST HAD been right. When I got up in the morning it was raining. It seemed kind of fitting that my last day walking should be in the rain.

I left the hut at about 11.30 a.m. It was about a 12-kilometre walk back to Halfmoon Bay. Strangely, after all this time, I wasn't in any hurry to get back.

Once I got going, the track was so easy. It was so well maintained that I didn't have to think about where I was putting my feet. There were even stairs up some of the steep bits. It was luxury! The track went up and over the hill to the signpost that I'd seen pointing towards North Arm 31 days ago. In that time, I'd managed to take in a huge part of the island, change my plans more than once, and learn a hell of a lot about myself.

When I got to the signpost, I turned and followed the arrow that pointed towards Halfmoon Bay. The last time I'd walked down this piece of track, I was scared, a bit unfit and completely out of touch with nature. That had all changed over the last month and so had I. While I mightn't have managed to achieve what I set out to do, I eventually managed to achieve the overall goal I set myself — I wanted to have fun and I had had a whole lot of it. I'd been true to myself and that was way more important to me than anything else.

The last seven days had been awesome. They hadn't been without hardship, but there had been a lot of fun in there as well. That's what adventures should be about.

This had been one of the greatest experiences ever. I learned more about myself than I had in the last year. I'd given myself some time to reflect on the whole adventure, which was so important as it meant that I'd already had time to process everything and to think about what I'd learned while I was out there.

As I walked towards the end of the track, I was thinking about ice cream and chocolate and all that good stuff. I was looking forward to getting to Oban, but there was one last surprise out on the track for me. As I walked, I saw someone coming towards me in a red and black check jacket. The guys from *Seven Sharp* were there to film me finishing. And they'd brought a little present for me — it was only my own Wildgirl, Ngaio.

I could barely believe my eyes. She'd told me that she couldn't get time off work to meet me so I didn't think I'd see her until I got back to the Coromandel. And here she was on Stewart Island! I was so surprised and so, so, *so* happy. It was the best surprise ever. It was better than all the ice cream, pizza and chocolate in the world.

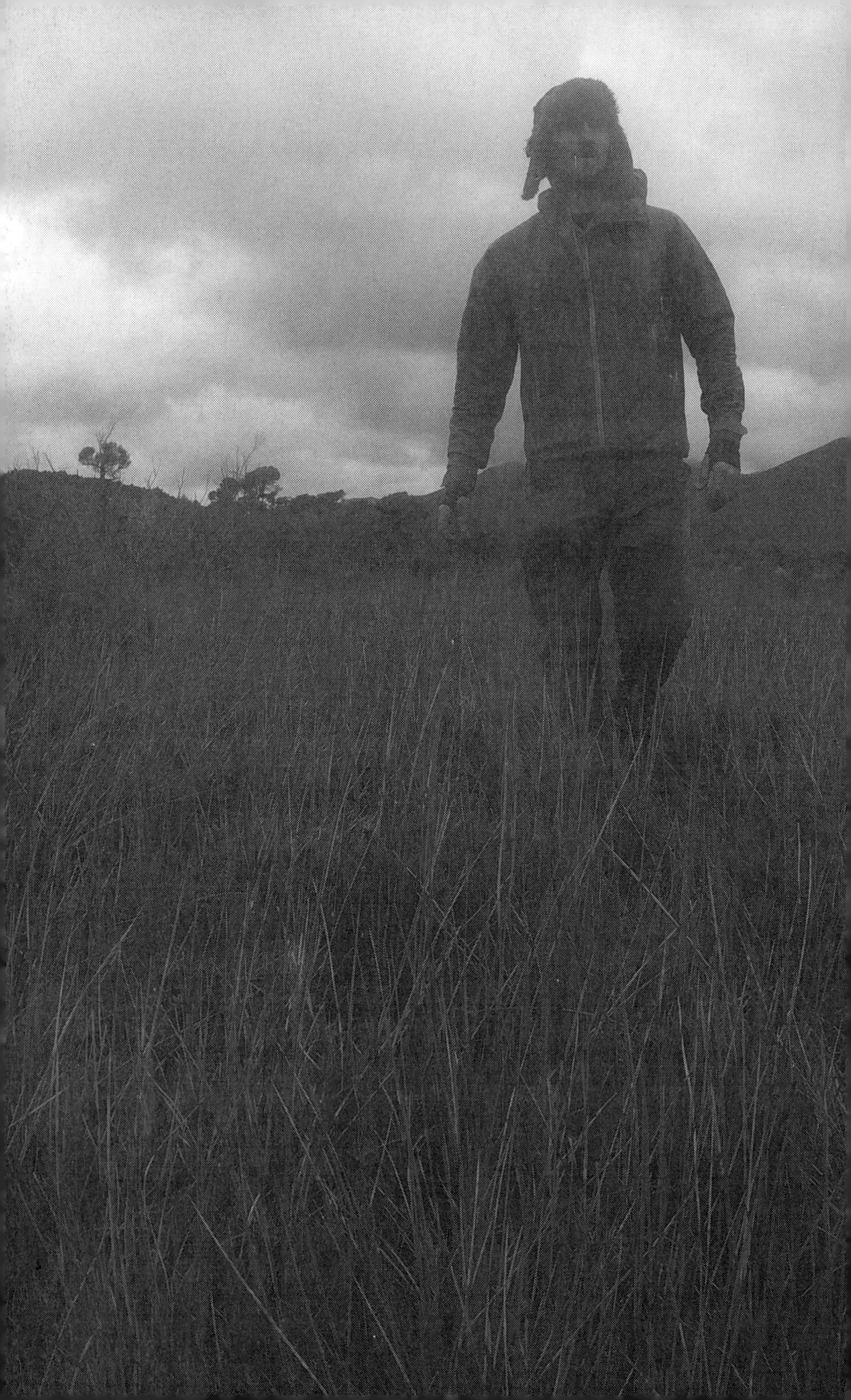

Chapter Twelve
AFTERWARDS

Finishing the walk, I was overwhelmed with Ngaio being there — and with food. So much food. I pretty much ate all the things I'd been dreaming about the whole time I'd been away. Ice cream, chocolate, chips . . . but then I'd throw up. The food was too different and there was too much of it. I had to eat — I couldn't *not* eat — I couldn't control the overpowering urge that I had to feed my body. But then I'd have to throw up. It was hard for my body and mind to adjust back to having food available all the time.

IT WAS SO GOOD to sleep in a bed again, but I found it made my body quite stiff and sore. All the aches and pains that my body had been fighting and hiding came to the fore as soon as I was comfortable! But it was so good to be clean and warm and full. And it was even better to be with my girl — even if it was only for one day because she had to get back to work.

The night after I'd finished the trip, I was in the pub and heaps of people came and asked me what I'd done. They were keen to see on the map where I'd been and what I'd been doing. It was great to be able to spin some yarns with them. I think they were happy that I'd got the island on *Seven Sharp* — especially because a new library was also opening, so they got TV coverage of that.

Stewart Island is different to anywhere else in New Zealand because the whole island is just one big community. Everyone knows everyone on the island. There's one school, three shops and only a couple of places to eat. I was amazed to see a French creperie and a pizza place. There's even a place that does foot massages for walkers. That was *so* good, although I did feel a bit bad for the poor lady who had to massage my messed-up feet!

I waved Ngaio off on the ferry the next morning, but I wasn't too sad because I knew that I would be home with her again really soon and I could talk to her whenever I wanted to.

I spent my last day visiting Ulva Island. It's part of the national park and is in Paterson Inlet. There are so many species of birds there and it's predator free. It's an amazing place — almost like Stewart Island in miniature.

The following morning, it was time for me to leave the island. I was on the 8 a.m. ferry back to Bluff, the mainland and 'real life'. There wasn't a cloud in the sky and the sun was already warm. I hoped it would be a smooth crossing, but on Foveaux Strait there are no guarantees. As we pulled out of Halfmoon Bay and into the open water, dolphins jumped alongside the boat.

I waved goodbye to the island. It had kicked my arse a couple of times but I was sad to be leaving — it really is a magical place.

I don't get seasick, but when I came back on that boat it

was horrendous. I was close to throwing up. I sat right on the front and I was on my phone the whole time, looking down. That was a mistake. It felt almost like I was drunk. I think part of that was because I'd been walking every day and had been on the ground, the feeling of being at sea was really weird. My balance was perfect for the ground then suddenly I was all over the place.

Arriving at Bluff, there was one last surprise for me. The kids from the local school were waiting outside the ferry terminal to do a haka for me. Then a couple of local guys came out and replied to the haka for me. I couldn't believe it. It was so humbling. What an incredible welcome back to the South Island.

MY EXPEDITION TOOK ME to some of the most wild and untouched landscapes I have been to. There were tough days, wet days, and moments when I thought I was going to give up. It was physically demanding and emotionally challenging. It was also full of the most inspiring views and a lot of bloody fantastic moments. It was one of those things you do in life that makes you a better person. It was full of real, raw life. Most of the time it was just me alone in a beautiful place.

Looking back on the whole trip now I realise just how much I learned about the world and about myself. I thought I knew all there was to know about me after my New Zealand trip but I had just scraped the surface.

I walked around New Zealand and that was meant to be my journey into manhood, the massive big adventure that changed my life. It did totally change my life — but it didn't give me the self-awareness and the self-reliance that I needed in order to make it in the world, so I had to go out there again.

The Stewart Island trip really opened my eyes to what's important to me. For so long I was trying to live in the light of being the first person to walk around New Zealand that I hadn't found out who I actually was. For a while, in my head, I was thinking, 'I'm better than that person and that person because I've walked around New Zealand.' That's not who I am at all, but without having had the opportunity to analyse myself I realised that that's what I'd become. I'd become one of those people who thought I was better than other people. That's so not the real me.

I was so focused on being an adventurer that I forgot that there were other things in my life. I was Wildboy, I had let that define me. I needed to get back to adventuring being something that I do rather than it being who I am. I wasn't Brando. I'd become a thing.

What made this trip so great was that it didn't go to plan. In my head I'd made myself way more brave and adventurous than I really was. I went to Stewart Island to get content for social media and to inspire people. I never really considered what I wanted out of the trip for myself.

I've discovered that I can be whoever I want to be. I can do whatever I want to do. I've discovered that the best person I can be is myself. You can create your own life, have a fancy car or no car. Wear nice clothes or go naked. Live in a mansion or in a tent . . . but the most important thing is that you are happy.

For a while, I thought life was about having cool things

and looking good. That's what I learnt growing up in the city — life's about looking good and pleasing others. Yes, you can look good but do it in your own style. Go out and be yourself and do what's right for you.

I've discovered the most amazing thing on this journey: it's not about doing something that's impossible or hardcore. It's about having fun and enjoying yourself. That's the secret. The message is do what makes you happy.

If you do what makes you happy, that's the secret to life. The only way to get there is by being yourself and owning who you are. Sure, you might face a few hurdles along the way, a few items might be lost, a few things might be missed out on, but the experience of losing them and the experience of figuring out how to deal with living without them is worth more than anything.

Do things because you want to do them, because you love doing them, because you love life. If you don't love your life, you're doing something wrong and you need to change it. It's as simple as that.

Acknowledgements

NOBODY ACHIEVES SUCCESS ALONE. I would like to thank Nic McCloy, the writer who helped me pull my story together. To all my friends and family, my Wildgirl, my agent, Kathmandu, GoPro, Absolute Wilderness: I couldn't do what I do today without your support. You have kept my dream alive, encouraged me when times have been tough, and helped me help others. Thank you all.

Wildboy
An epic trek around the coast of New Zealand

Brando 'Wildboy' Yelavich's whirlwind tour of the coastline of New Zealand. Extreme adventure, near misses, good sorts, and one beautiful country — *Wildboy* has it all!

His life fast going off the rails, Brando Yelavich decided he needed to change his path. He needed a mission. He was going to walk around New Zealand.

Brando reached Cape Reinga on 23 August 2014 after a gruelling journey of over 8000 kilometres, traversed almost completely on foot over 600 days — the first time it had ever been done.

It was an outlandish odyssey of physical and mental fortitude. He slept under the stars and lived off the land. He almost drowned on several occasions and experienced near-hypothermia. But the impact ran much deeper.

For fans of Bear Grylls, Cheryl Strayed's *Wild* and the off-the-grid outdoors Kiwi experience, *Wildboy* is a ripping adventure story with an inspiring life change at its heart.

Also available as an ebook